WHAT IT WILL TAKE TO CHANGE THE WORLD

WHAT IT WILL TAKE TO CHANGE THE WORLD

S. D. Gordon

Edited and Abridged by
DICK EASTMAN

Introduction by
JACK McALISTER
Founder/President of
World Literature Crusade

BAKER BOOK HOUSE
Grand Rapids, Michigan

ISBN: 0-8010-3746-8
Printed in the United States of America

This book, originally published in 1908 under the title *Quiet Talks with World Winners*, was edited and abridged by Dick Eastman, Director of the Change the World School of Prayer, sponsored by World Literature Crusade, P.O. Box 1313, Studio City, California, 91604. WLC is a world-wide ministry that provides free gospel literature to over 415 denominations and missionary groups across the world. They systematically distribute this literature house-to-house in villages and towns. For further information about this ministry, or about when a Change the World School of Prayer training program will be conducted in your area, write to the above address.

Contents

Introduction

Jack McAlister
Founder/President of World Literature Crusade

Almost three quarters of a century have passed since S. D. Gordon took his pen in hand and sketched the brief outlines that eventually became chapters of this meaningful book. Yet, Gordon's insight into the cry of the Master's heart for world evangelism is as alive and pertinent today—if not more so—as when he first wrote these words.

As S. D. Gordon firmly reminds us, Jesus came to earth for a single purpose—to die on a cross to set men free from sin. Likewise, following His glorious resurrection, this same Jesus commissioned His disciples to accomplish a single purpose—carry the good news of His resurrection victory to every person on earth. No one is to be missed. We are to go into "all the world" and reach "every creature" (Mark 16:15).

Herein lies the problem that S. D. Gordon

addresses on the following pages: "Has the Christian church failed or succeeded in fulfilling this commission?" The answer is sadly obvious. More than nineteen centuries have passed since Christ commanded His followers to fulfil this single objective, and yet almost half the world still waits to hear or read of a loving Savior.

That is not to say the church in America and other free nations has failed to impress a secularized society with its advances in certain areas. No age in Christendom has witnessed greater church programs than the present. Here in our nation million-dollar church sanctuaries are not at all uncommon, in even the smallest of denominations. I've counted no fewer than twenty such edifices located within a thirty-mile radius of my home alone.

Then, too, media advances have also been spectacular—at least in the amount of dollars spent. The prestigious *Wall Street Journal* recently reported that American churches, alone, spent one-half *billion* dollars on television programing in a single year; this money was directed primarily toward a further saturation of our nation with the gospel.

In recent months three major evangelical ministries in the United States have announced building programs with budgets in excess of 100 million dollars—for hospitals, Christian conference centers, universities, and a host of other planned programs; all of this money is slated for development *within* the boundaries of our already richly blessed nation.

Although we thank God for His blessings on a growing church here at home, we cannot help but wonder what it will take to bring Christ's love to the overseas peoples of the world—the vast majority of whom live daily under a dark cloud of political and spiritual repression.

Could it be that the church in America has failed to establish true priorities in the matter of world evangelism? A recent article by Don Hillis in *Christianity Today* (May, 1977) provides this statistical answer to our question:

1. The United States has more ordained ministers (330,000) than there are in all other countries of the world combined, although some 94% of the world's population lives beyond the borders of the United States.
2. We have more Christian radio stations and more hours of Gospel broadcasting (radio and television) than all the rest of the world together. And in addition to these numerous Christian stations, some 6,000 different secular radio stations air one or more Gospel broadcasts every week. In Los Angeles, California, alone there are more than 4,100 religious radio broadcasts every month, and more than 350 hours of Christian television broadcasts each week.
3. We have 60,000 young people in our Bible Colleges and tens of thousands more in Christian liberal arts colleges—more than the rest of the world combined.
4. On any given Sunday more people attend Sunday Schools in the United States than the total attendance of all Sunday Schools

of the remaining 209 countries of the world—together.

5. Although 94% of the world's population lives beyond our borders, more than 90% of every dollar given in our church offerings is spent here in our country; in spite of the fact that almost half the world has never had a witness of the resurrected Christ, and 7 out of 8 *Christians* in the world have never owned a complete Bible.

What will it take to change these statistics—and ultimately, the world? First, we must allow God to impress upon us the significance of Christ's statement in Matthew 13:38, "The field is the world!" My community—with its scores of evangelical churches—is only a *part* of that world. It is not *the* world. To pray for (and give to) God's work only in my community is to ignore the vastness of Christ's total world. Beyond that, it is spiritually selfish.

Then, too, we must seek to become involved in a meaningful plan that will actually change our world—a plan that will give the gospel to every creature everywhere. We must firmly reject all denominational arguing and theological hair-splitting that so often hinder the advance of God's work. Christ's gospel is simple, and our plan to share His gospel also must be simple.

S. D. Gordon discussed the framework of this plan in these words:

> The great concern now is to make Jesus fully known to all mankind. That is the plan. It is a simple plan. Men who have been changed are

> to be world-changers. Nobody else can be. The warm enthusiasm of grateful love must burn in the heart and drive all the life. There must be simple, but thorough organization.
>
> The campaign should be mapped out as thoroughly as a presidential campaign is organized in America. The purpose of a presidential campaign is really stupendous in its object and sweep. It is to influence quickly, up to the point of decisive action, the individual opinion of millions of men, spread over millions of square miles, and that, too, in the face of a vigorous opposing campaign to influence them the other way. The whole country is mapped out and organized on broad lines and into the smallest details.
>
> . . . We need as thorough organizing, as aggressive enthusiasm, and as intelligent planning for this great task which our Master has put into our hands.

Although these words by S. D. Gordon were already out of print for many years when World Literature Crusade began in 1946, it was on these very principles that the ministry began. When a country was selected for total evangelization, available Christians were mobilized, along with trained full-time distributors, to systematically reach every home of every town and village. Because of the emphasis to reach every home of an area, the overseas name for World Literature Crusade became "Every Home Crusade." Today, fifty major offices have been strategically established throughout the world, employing over 3,000 workers who combine their efforts with thousands of volunteers from more than 415 denominations and missionary groups. They work together to place the printed gospel of Jesus Christ in the homes of more than one million people every day. To date, gospel literature has been delivered to homes where more than 1,700,000,000 people live—two of every five homes on earth. By next year half of all the homes on earth will have received the printed message of Christ's love.

All literature is distributed systematically, house to house, so that every person has access to the message. A gospel booklet for both children and adults is placed in each home. Wherever people live, distributors go. Because not everyone lives at home, specialized distribution programs take the Good News to hospitals, universities, prisons, and every busy seaport where seamen spend a few days' leave before returning to their ships for weeks or months at sea. For the blind, the gospel is distributed in Braille, and for those totally unable to read, portable, hand-operated record players—not much larger than the size of this book—announce the message of Christ's love. (One thriving church in northern India, with over 160 members, began when a twelve-year-old Hindu lad found Christ while listening to a portable gospel recording.)

Attached to each piece of literature is a special preaddressed decision card. In a recent twelve-month period, 1,442,314 cards were received in our fifty overseas offices. Each new convert was enrolled in a four-lesson Bible Correspondence Course, and—whenever possible—the new convert was channeled into a nearby church. Of necessity, however, many must receive their inspiration from printed devotional matter or in small groups of new Christians (called "Christ Groups") because the nearest church is well beyond traveling distance.

But all of these statistics concern only the "practics" of the plan—how it functions and a few results. Far more significant is the "power" behind the plan. *Prayer makes it all happen.* In the past several years more than 100,000 Christians of almost 100 denominations have attended the Change the World School of Prayer, an eight-hour prayer training program sponsored by World Literature Crusade. These participants have learned how to change the course of history through their praying, and the record shows it is making a difference. Almost 80,000 Christians have pledged to pray one hour each day, blanketing God's work with 560,000 hours of prayer every week. Little wonder the harvest of written decisions through the distribution of gospel literature reached an average of as many as 6,294 per day in one recent month.

Beloved believer, it is possible to change the world, but not without your personal involvement. It is true that some of the task might be accomplished without you, but a portion of the work—perhaps the evangelization of some distant province of China or a peasant village in Eastern Europe—will go untouched without your involvement.

So, as you read the pages of this remarkable

little book, bear in mind that you have been commissioned as a world-changer. Christ clearly meant for all of His followers—including you and me—to literally fulfil His command to give the gospel to every creature. It is not an impossible task. God has given us a workable plan. The job can be done!

And wherever barriers arise that seemingly shut off a nation from the knowledge of Christ's love, our prayers will combine in awesome power to crush those troublesome barriers. Mountains will be moved and every enemy destroyed. Together, in a spirit of prayer and sacrifice, *we will change the world!*

1

The Master's Passion

Calvary in Genesis

There is a great passion burning in the heart of God. It is tenderly warm and tenaciously strong. Its fires never burn low, nor lose their fine glow. That passion is to win man back home again. The whole world of man is included in its warm, eager reach.

The old home hearth-fire of God is lonely since man went away. The family circle is broken. God will not rest until that old home circle is complete again, and every voice joins in the home songs.

It is an *overmastering* passion, the overmastering passion of God's heart. It has guided and controlled all His thoughts and plans for man from the first. The purpose of winning man, and the whole race, back again is the dominant gripping passion of God's heart today. Everything is made to bend to this one end.

When Eden's tragedy came to darken the earliest pages of the Bible, and, far worse, to darken the pages of human life, there was a great glimpse of this passion of God's heart in the guarding of Eden's gates. The presence of the angels with their sword of flame told plainly of a day when man would be coming back again to the old Eden home of God. The place must be carefully guarded for him.

This is a *love* passion, a passion of love. And love itself is the master passion both of the human heart and of God's heart. Nothing can grip and fill and sway the heart either of man or God like that.

We would all easily agree that the greatest picture of God's marvelous, overmastering passion of love is seen in the cross. All men as they have come to know that story have stood with heads bowed and bared before the love revealed there. They have not understood it. They have quarreled about its meaning. But they have acknowledged its love and power as beyond that of any other story or picture.

However men may differ as to why Jesus died, and how His dying affects us, they all agree that the scene of the cross is the greatest revelation of love ever known or ever shown. All theories of the atonement seem to be lost sight of in one thought of grateful acknowledgment of a stupendous love, as men are drawn together by the magnetism of the hilltop of Calvary.

But there is a wondrously clear foreshadowing of that tremendous cross scene in the earliest page of the Bible. Nowhere is love, God's passion of love, made to stand out more distinctly and vividly than in the first chapter of Genesis. The afterscene of the cross uses more intense coloring—the blacks are inkier in their blackness; the reds deeper and redder; the contrasts sharper to the startling-point—yet there is nothing in the story of the cross as found in the Gospels which is not included fully in this first leaf of revelation. But it has taken the light of the cross to open our eyes to see how much is plainly there. Let us look at it more closely.

The Love Passion

What is this greatest of passions called love? There is no word harder to get a satisfactory definition of. Because, whatever you say about it, there comes quickly to your mind someone who loves you, or you think of the passion that burns in your own heart for someone. And, as you think of that, no words that anybody may use seem at all strong enough, or tender enough, to tell what love is, as you know it in your own inner heart.

Yet I think this much can be said—love is the tender, strong outgoing of your whole being to another. It is a passion burning like a fire within you, a soft-burning but intense fire within you, for some other one. Every mention of that name stirs the flame into new burning. Every lingering thought of him or her is like fresh air making the flames leap up more eagerly. And each personal contact is a clearing out of all the ashes, and a turning on of all the draughts, to feed new oxygen for stronger, fresher burning.

There are many other things that seem like love. Kindliness and friendliness, and even more intense emotions, use love's name for themselves. But though these have likenesses to love, they are not love. They have caught something of its warm glow. A bit of the high coloring of its flames plays on them. But they are not the real thing, only distant kinsfolk. The severe tests of life quickly reveal their lack.

Love itself is really an aristocrat. It allows very, very few into its inner circle, often only one. The real thing of love is never selfish. Now we know very well that in the thick of life the fine gold of love gets mixed up with the baser metals. It is very often overlaid and shot through with much that is mean and low. Rank selfishness, both the coarse kind and the refined, cultured sort, seeks a hiding place under its cloak. But the stuff mixed in it is not love, but a defiling of it. That defiling is a bit of the slander love suffers for a time, from the presence in life of sin.

Weeds with their poison, and snakes and spiders with their deadly venom, draw life from the sun. That is a matter of the bad transmuting the good, pure sun into its own sort. The sun itself never produces poison or any hurtful thing.

Love itself is never mean, nor bad, nor selfish. The man who truly loves the woman whom he would have for his own lifelong, closest companion is not selfish. He does not want her chiefly for his own sake, but for her sake, that he may guard and care for her, and that her life may fully grow in the sunlight of the love it must have. And, if you think that is idealizing love out of all practical reach, please remember that true love will steadily refuse any union that would not be best for the loved one.

What is the finest and highest love that we know? There are many different sorts and degrees of love revealed in man's relation with his fellows: conjugal, the love between husband and wife; paternal, the love of a father for his child; maternal, the mother's love for her child; filial, the love of children for father and mother; fraternal, or brotherly, meaning really the love of children of the same parents for each other, both brothers and sisters—the same word is used for love between friends where there is no tie of blood; and patriotic, or love for one's country. And under that last word may be loosely grouped the love that one may have for any special object, to which he may devote his life, outside of personal relationships, such as music or any profession or occupation.

This is putting the sorts of love in their logical order. Though in our experience we know the father- and mother-love for ourselves first; and then in turn the others, so far as they come to us, until we must complete the circle and reach the climax of father- and mother-love in ourselves going out to our own children.

Mother-Love

Now of these sorts and degrees, which is the highest and finest? Well, your answer to that question will depend entirely on your own experience, as every answer and every thought we have of everything does. All children have mothers, or have had, but thousands of children do not know a mother's love.

I was speaking one time in New York City about the conception, of which the Bible is so full, that God is a mother. And the English evangelist, Gipsy Smith, who lost his mother when very young, but who had an unusually devoted father, said with charming simplicity that he could not see how God could be called just a mother, but he knew He was a father. And then he went on to speak very winsomely of God as a father.

Many times love is not born in the heart at all, until there comes into the life someone outside of one's own kin. Many a woman never knows love until it is awakened in her heart by him who henceforth is to be a part of herself.

But the common answer, that most people everywhere give to the question, is that a *mother's love* is the greatest human love we know. And if you press them to tell why they think so, the most frequent answer is that she gives so much of herself. She gives her very life. If need be, she sacrifices everything in life, and then sacrifices life itself, going out into the darkness of death that her child may come into fulness and sweetness of life. This is the mother spirit, giving one's very self to bring life to another.

The mother gives her very lifeblood that the new life may come. And, if need be, she will gladly give her life *out* to death that the new life may come into life. And yet more, she gives her life out daily and yearly, throughout its length, so the full strength and fragrance of life may come into her child's life.

Yet, when all this has been said, I am strongly inclined to think that the mother's love, though the greatest that can be found in any one heart, is not the perfect, fully grown love. The fundamental human unit is not a man nor a woman, but a man *and* a woman. Perfect love requires more than one or two for its matured growth into full life. It cannot exist in its full strength and fragrant sweets except where three are joined together to draw out its full depth and meaning.

There must be two whose hearts are fully joined in love, each finding, answering and ever-satisfying love in the other, each love thus growing to full ripeness in the warm sunshine of the other love. And then there needs to be a third one, who comes as a result of that mutual love, and who constantly draws out the love of the other two.

For love in itself is creative. It yearns to bring into being another upon whom it may freely lavish itself. That other one must be of its own sort, upon its own level. Nothing less ever satisfies. And so the love poured out draws out to itself an answering love fully as full as its own. And then, having yearned, it does more. It creates. It must create. It must bring forth life, and life like its own in all its powers and privileges. This is the very life of love in its full expression.

Yet to say all this is simply to spell out fully, in all its letters and syllables, the great, the greatest of passions, mother-love, which we agreed a moment ago is the highest. For mother-love is not restricted to woman, though among us humans it often finds its brightest expressions in her. It knows no restriction of sex. It is simply love at its fullest and highest and freest and tenderest; it is love free to do as it will, and to do it as fully as it will. Love left to itself, free to do as its heart dictates, will give its very self, its life, that life may come to another. This is the great passion called love, the greatest of all passions.

The Genesis Picture

Now, maybe you think we have swung far away from the first chapter of the Genesis revelation. No; you are mistaken there. We have been walking, with rapid stride, by the shortest road, straight into its inner heart. Let us look a bit at the picture of God sketched for us in this earliest page of revelation.

There are two creations here, first of the earth, man's home; and then of man himself who was to live in the home. Here at once in the beginning is mother-love. Before the new life comes the mother is absorbed in getting the home ready; she aims at the best and softest and homiest home that her mother-love can think of, and her fingers can fix. The same mother instinct in the birds spends itself in getting the nest ready, and then patiently broods until the new occupants come to take possession.

The Bible never calls God a mother, though maternal language, as here, is used of Him many times. It takes more of the human to tell the divine. You must take many words, and several of our human relationships, and put them together, in the finest meaning of each, to get near the full meaning of what God is. Up on the higher level, with God, the word *father* really includes all that both father and mother mean to us.

The word *father* is even used once of God in what we think of as strictly a maternal sense. In speaking of God's early care of the Hebrews, Paul says, "as a *nursing-father* bore he them in the wilderness" (Acts 13:18, American Revised). That word *nursing-father* is peculiar in coupling the distinctive function of the mother in caring for the babe with the word *father*.

The word *father* applied to God includes not only our meaning of father in all its strength as we know it at its best, but all of the meaning of the word *mother*, in all its sweet fragrance, as we have had it breathed into our own very life.

We have come commonly to think of the word

mother as a tenderer word than *father*. Yet I have met many, both men and women, who unconsciously revealed that their experience has made father the tenderer (even the tenderest) word to them. Father stands commonly for the stronger, more rugged qualities; and mother for the finer, gentler, sweeter, maybe softer qualities, in the strong meaning of that word *soft*.

God Giving Himself

Here in this Genesis story the creation of the whole sun-system to give life to the earth, and of the earth itself, was the outward beginning of this greatest passion of love in the heart of God. And if you would know more of that love in this early stage of it, just look a bit at the home itself. It has been rather badly mussed, soiled, and hurt by sin's foul touch. Yet even so it is a wonder of a world in its beauty and fruitfulness. What must it have been before the slime and tangle of sin got in! But that is a whole story by itself. We must not stop there just now.

When the home was ready God set Himself to bringing the new life He was planning. And He did it, even as father and mother of our human kind and of every other kind do: He gave some of Himself. He breathed into man His own life-breath. He came Himself, and with the warmth and vitality of His life brought a new life. The new life was a bit of Himself.

That phrase, "breathed into his nostrils,"

brings to us the conception of the closest personal, physical contact—two together in most intimate contact, and life passing from one to the other. The picture of Elijah stretching his warm body upon that of the widow's son until the life-breath came again comes instinctively to mind. And its companion scene comes with it, of Elisha lying prone upon the child, mouth to mouth, eye to eye, hand to hand, until the breath again softly re-entered that little, precious body.

And if all this seems too plain and homely a way to talk about the great God, let us remember that is the way of this blessed old Book. It is the only way we shall come to know the marvelous intimacy and tenderness of God's love, and of God's touch upon ourselves.

How shall we talk best about God so as to get clear, sensible ideas about Him? Why not follow the rule of the old Bible? Can we do better? It constantly speaks of Him in the language that we use of men. The scholars, with their fondness for big words, say the Bible is anthropomorphic. That simply means that it uses man's words and man's ideas of things in telling about God. It makes use of the common words and ideas, that man understands fully, to tell about the God whom he does not know. Could there be a more sensible way? Indeed, how else could man understand?

Some dear, godly people have sometimes been afraid of the use of simple, homely language in talking about God. To speak of Him in the common language of everyday life, the common talk of home and kitchen, and shop and street and trade, seems to them lacking in due reverence. Do they forget that simple language is the language of the common people? And of our good old Anglo-Saxon Bible? Has anybody ever yet used as blunt, homely talk as this old Book uses? And has any other book struck into people's memories and hearts with such burrlike hold as it has?

That breathing by God into man's nostrils of the breath of life suggests the most intense concentration of strength and thought and heart. The whole heart of God went out to man in that breath that brought life.

God's Fellow

The whole thought of God's heart was that man be *like Himself.* Over and over again, with all the peculiar emphasis of repetition, it is said that the man was to be in the very image, or likeness, of God. God gave Himself that the man might be a bit of Himself. Here is the love-passion, the mother-passion, the father-mother-passion, in its highest mood, and doing its own finest work.

The man was to be the very best, that he might have fellowship of the most intimate sort with God. Of course, only those who are alike can have fellowship. Only in that particular thing which any two have in common can they have fellowship together. Let me use a common word in its old, fine, first meaning: man was made to be God's *fellow,* His most intimate associate and companion.

As you read this early story in Genesis of God's passion of love, you know, if you stop to think of it, that if ever the need came, He would climb any Calvary hill, however steep, and receive the jagging nails of any cross, however cutting, for the sake of His darling child—man.

This love-passion never fails. There is no emergency that can arise that is too great for love's resources. Any danger, however great, every need, no matter how distressing, is already provided for by love. The emergency may sorely test and tax love to its last limit, but it can never outdo it, nor outstrip it in the race. No matter how great the danger, love is a bit greater. No matter how strong the enemy threatening, love is always yet stronger. However deep down into the very vitals of life the poison sting may sink its fangs, love goes yet deeper, neutralizing the deadly influence with its own fresh lifeblood.

Have you ever looked into a single drop of water and seen the sun—the whole of that brilliant ball of fire there in one tiny drop of water? Well, there's one word on this first leaf of the Book which contains the clear reflection, sharply outlined, of the whole creation story; ah! yes, more than that, of the whole gospel story.

Come here and look; you can see in its clear surface the form of a man climbing a little, steep hill, and being hung, thorn-crowned, upon a cross of pain and shame. In Genesis 1:2 is the word *brooding*. The King James, the English Revised, and American Revised have the word *moved*. The Revisions add *brooding* in the margin. And that is the root meaning of the original Hebrew word—*brooding*, or rendered more fully, "was brooding tremulous with love."

God's Watermark

That English word *brooding*, as well as the Hebrew word underneath, is a mother word. The brooding hen sits so faithfully, day after day, upon the eggs, bringing the new lives by the vital warmth of her own body. The mother bird nestles softly down upon the nest in the crotch of the tree, patiently, expectantly brooding, by the strength of her own life giving life to the coming young. She who, in the holiest, greatest function entrusted to her, comes nearest to God in creative power and love—the mother of our human kind—broods for long months over her coming child, giving her very life, until the crisis of birth comes; and then broods still, for months and years longer, that the new life may come into fulness of life. That is the great word used here.

Now, will you please notice very keenly the connection in which the word occurs. It was because the earth was "waste and void, and darkness upon the face of the deep," that the Spirit of God was brooding. It is only fair to say that our scholarly friends who know Hebrew are divided as to the meaning here. Some think that these words, "waste and void," simply indicate a stage, or step, in the processes of creation.

But others are just as positive in saying that the words point plainly to a disaster of some sort that took place. In their view the whole story of creation is in the ten opening words of the chapter. Then follows a bad break of some sort; then the brooding of God in verse two; and the rest of the chapter is taken up in what is practically a reshaping up again of the whole affair. Some of this second group of Hebrew scholars have made this translation, "The earth became a waste," or "a wreck," or "a ruin," or "without inhabitant."

This reading gives a world of additional meaning to the word "*brooding*." Here was love not merely giving life, but giving itself to overcome a disaster. The brooding was to mend a break. Love creates. It also redeems. It stoops down with great patience, and washes the dirt and filth thoroughly off, in the best cleansing liquid to be found, and brings the cleansed, redeemed man back again.

Love does indeed create. It gave man the power to choose freely, without any restriction, whatever he would choose to choose. Redeeming love does more. It woos him to choose the right, and only the right. It gets down by his side after his eyesight has become twisted, and his will badly kinked by wrong choosing, and patiently, persistently works to draw him up to the level of choosing right. Love makes us like God in the power of choice. But there is a greater task ahead. It makes us yet more like Him in the desire to choose only the right, and in the power to choose it too. All this is in that marvelous world of a word—*brooding*.

The whole story of the sacrifice of Calvary is included in this wondrous first leaf of revelation. If we had lost the Gospels, and did not know their story, not the history of man, we yet could know from this Genesis page that, if ever the need arose, God would lavishly give out His very life, at any cost of suffering and pain, that His man might be saved. John 3:16 is in the first chapter of Genesis. Calvary is in the creation. God gave His breath to man in creation, and His blood for man on Calvary. He gave His blood because He had given His breath. Each was His very life.

You know the way publishers have of putting an imprint in a book by means of what is called a watermark. By the skilful use of water in manufacturing the paper, a name or trade imprint is made a part of the very paper of which the book is made.

Have you ever noticed God's watermark on the paper of this first leaf of His Book? Hold your Bible up; separate this first leaf and hold it up to the light and try to see through it. The best light to use is that which comes from Calvary. Can you see the watermark plainly imprinted there? Look closely and carefully for it is there. In clearcut outline, every bit of it showing sharply, is a cross. And if you look still more closely, you will find this watermark different from those in common use, in this—*there is a distinct blood-red tinge to it.*

A Picture of God

Illustrations of God from our common life are never full, and must not be taken too critically, but they are sometimes wonderfully vivid and very helpful. Anything that makes God seem real and near helps.

A few years ago I heard a simple story of real life from the lips of a New England clergyman. It was told of a brother clergyman of the same denomination who was stationed in the same city.

This clergyman had a son, about fourteen years of age, who, of course, was going to school. One day the boy's teacher called at the house and asked for the father. When they met, he said—

"Is your son sick?"

"No; why?"

"He was not at school today."

"You don't mean it!"

"Nor yesterday."

"Indeed!"

"Nor the day before."

"Well!"

"And I supposed he was sick."

"No, he's not sick."

"Well, I thought I should tell you."

After receiving the father's thanks, the teacher left. The father sat thinking about his son, and those three days. By and by he heard a click at the gate, and he knew the boy was coming in. So he went to the door to meet him at once. And the boy knew as he looked up that the father knew about those three days.

The father said, "Come into the library, Phil." Phil went and the door was shut.

Then the father said very quietly, "Phil, your teacher was here a little while ago. He tells me you were not at school today, nor yesterday, nor the day before. And we thought you were. You let us think you were. And you don't know how bad I feel about this. I have always said I could trust my boy Phil. I always have trusted you. And here you have been a living lie for three whole days. I can't tell you how bad I feel about it."

Well, it was hard on the boy to be talked to in that gentle way. If his father had spoken to him roughly, or had taken him out to the woodshed, in the rear of the dwelling, it wouldn't have been nearly so hard.

Then the father said, "We'll get down and pray." And the thing was getting harder for Phil all the time. He didn't want to pray just then. Most people don't in similar circumstances.

They got down on their knees, side by side. The father poured out his heart in prayer. And the boy listened. Somehow he saw himself in the looking glass of his knee joints as he had not before. It is odd about the mirror of the knee joints, the things you see in it. Most people do not like to use it much. As they got up from their knees, the father's eyes were wet, and Phil's eyes were not dry.

Then the father said, "My boy, there's a law of life, that where there is sin there is suffering. You can't get those two things apart. Wherever there is suffering there has been sin, somewhere, by somebody. And wherever there is sin there will be suffering, for someone, somewhere; and likely most for those closest to you."

"Now," he said, "my boy, you have done wrong. So we'll do this. You go upstairs to the attic. I'll make a little bed for you there in the corner. We'll bring your meals up to you at the usual times. And you stay up in the attic three days and three nights, as long as you've been a living lie." The boy did not say a word. They climbed the attic steps. The father kissed his boy, and left him alone.

Suppertime came, and the father and mother sat down to eat. But they could not eat for thinking of their son. The longer they chewed on the food, the bigger and drier it got in their mouths. And swallowing was clearly out of the question. The mother said, "Why don't you eat?" And the father replied softly, "Well, why don't *you* eat?" And, with a catch in her throat, she said, "I can't, for thinking of Phil." And he said, "That's what's bothering me."

They rose from the supper table, and went into the sitting room. He took up the evening paper, and she began sewing. His eyesight was not very good. He wore glasses, and tonight they seemed to blur up. He could not see the print distinctly.

It must have been the glasses, of course. So he took them off, and wiped them with great care, and then found the paper was upside down. And she tried to sew. But the thread broke, and she could not seem to get the thread into the needle again. How we all reveal ourselves in just such details!

By and by the clock struck ten, their usual hour of retiring. But they made no move to go. The mother said quietly, "Aren't you going to bed?" And he said, "I'm not sleepy, I think I'll sit up a while longer; you go." "No, I guess I'll wait a while too." And the clock struck eleven; then the hands clicked around close to twelve. And they arose, and went to bed—but not to sleep. Each one pretended to be asleep. And each knew the other was not asleep.

After a while she said—woman is always the keener—"Why aren't you asleep?" He replied softly, "How did you know I wasn't sleeping? Why don't you go to sleep?" And she said, with that same odd catch in her voice, "I can't, for thinking of Phil." He said, "That's what's wrong with me." And the clock struck one; and then two; still no sleep. At last the father said, "Mother, I can't stand this. *I'm going upstairs with Phil.*"

And he took his pillow, went softly out of the room, climbed the attic steps softly, and pressed the latch softly so as not to wake the boy if he were asleep. He tiptoed across to the corner by the window. There the boy lay, wide awake, with something glistening in his eyes, and what looked like stains on his cheeks. The father got down between the sheets, and they put their arms around each other's necks, for they had always been the best of friends, and their tears got mixed up on each other's cheeks—you could not have told which were the father's and which the son's. Then they slept together until the morning light broke.

When sleep time came the second night, the father said, "Good night, Mother. I'm going up with Phil again." And the second night he shared his boy's punishment in the attic. And the third night when sleep time came, again he said, "Mother, good night. I'm going up with the boy." And the third night he shared his son's punishment with him.

That boy, now a man grown, in the height of his strength, my acquaintance told me, is telling the story of Jesus with tongue of flame and life of flame as a missionary out in the heart of China.

Do you know, I think that is the best picture of God I have ever run across in any gallery of life? It is not a perfect picture. No human picture of God is perfect, except, of course, what we know of Him in the person of Jesus. The boy's punishment was arbitrarily chosen by the father, unlike God's dealings with our sin. But this story is the tenderest and most real human picture of God of any that has come to me.

God could not take away sin. It is here. Very plainly it is here. And He could not take away suffering, out of kindness to us. For suffering is sin's index finger pointing out danger. It is sin's voice calling loudly, "Look out! there's something wrong." So He came down in the person of His Son, Jesus, and lay down alongside of man for three days and nights, in the place where sin drove man.

That is God! And that suggests graphically the great passion of His heart. Sin was not ignored. Its lines stood sharply out. The boy in the attic had two things burned into his memory, never to be erased: *the wrong of his own sin, and the strength of his father's love.*

Jesus is God coming down into our midst and giving His own very life, and then, more, giving it out in death, that He might make us hate sin, and might woo and win the whole world, away from sin, back to the intimacies of the old family circle again.

Jesus, the Lover

Jesus was a mirror held up to the Father's face for man to look into. So we may know what the Father is like. When you look at Jesus and listen to Him, you are looking into the Father's heart and listening to its warm throbbing. And no one can look there without being caught by the great passion burning there, and feeling its intense soft-burning glow, and carrying some of it forever after in his own heart.

Jesus was on a *wooing errand* to the earth. He came to change the world! The whole spirit of

His dealings with men was that of a great lover, wooing them to the Father. He was insistently eager to let men know what His Father is like. He seemed jealous of His Father's reputation among men. It had been slandered badly. Men misunderstood the Father. Jesus would leave no stone unturned to let men know how good and loving and winsome God is. For then they would eagerly run back home again to Him. This was His method of approach to the world He came to win.

Jesus is the greatest wooer the old world has ever known, and will be the greatest winner of what He is after, too. Run thoughtfully through the Gospels, and stand by Jesus' side in each one of these simple, tremendous incidents of His contact with the common people. Then listen anew to His teaching talks, so homely and so powerful. And the impression becomes irresistible that the one thought that gripped His heart at every turn, never forgotten, was to woo man back to allegiance to the Father.

Christ's World-Passion

Have you not marked *the worldwide swing* of our Master's thought and plan? It is stupendous in its freshness and bold daring. His idea of the thing to be done was immense. To use a favorite phrase of today, He had a *world-consciousness*. It is hard for us to realize what a startling thing

His world-consciousness was. We are so well-acquainted with the Gospels that we lose much of their force through mere rote of familiarity.

It takes a determined effort, and the fresh touch of the Holy Spirit, too, to have the Gospels come with all the freshness of a new book. And then in our day, and in our part of the world especially, we have become used to talking about worldwide enterprises.

We do not realize what a stupendous thing a world-consciousness was in Jesus' day. He certainly did not get it from His own generation, not from the Jews. It stands out in keen contrast to their ideas. They lived within very narrow alleyways. They supposed they were the favorites of God, and that everybody else was a *dog*, and a *damned* dog, too (not in the profane usage, but actually).

But Jesus thought of the *world*, and yearned for the world. The words *world* and *earth* were constantly on His lips. He said that He came "into the world," not to Palestine; that was only the door He used for entrance. It was from Jesus that John learned (what he later wrote down) that He was to "lighten *every man* that cometh into *the world*."

To the Jewish senator of the inner national circle Jesus said plainly in that great sentence that contains the gift of the whole Bible—John 3:16—that it was the *world* He was after. A *saved world* was the one purpose of His errand to the earth. He had come to save the world (John

3:17), and would stop at nothing short of giving His very self "for the life of *the world*."

Jesus told His own inner circle that the field was the *world*. And that it was to be won by the means He Himself was using; namely, men, human beings, "sons of the kingdom" (Matt. 13:38), were to be sown as seed all over its vast extent.

Do you remember that during Jesus' last week the Greeks requested an interview (John 12:20–33)? The outside, non-Jewish world came to Him in that earnest request of those Greeks. And His whole being became greatly agitated. It was as when one, at last, after years of labor without any seeming success, gets a first faint glimpse of the results he longs so earnestly for. Here was a touch, a glimpse of the very thing on which His heart was so set. The great outside world was coming to Him.

Realization of the tremendous meaning of the Greeks' request, the sure promise it held of the day when *all the world would be coming*, seems to set Him all a-tremble with intensest emotion. The delight of the possible realizing of His life dream and His earth errand, and yet the terrific conviction that only by traveling the red road of the cross could that world be won, made a fierce conflict within. It was a vision for a lost world that agitated Him.

And it was that same vision that held Him steady. He would not waver. By concentrating all in one act He would generate and set off a dynamic power on Calvary that would shake and then change a world. The knowledge that all men would be irresistibly drawn by the loadstone of the cross steadied His steps.

A few days later, as He sat resting on the side of the Hill of Olivet, the disciples earnestly asked for some idea of His plan. And He explained that the gospel was to be "preached to the *whole inhabited* earth" (Matt. 24:14). That conception was never out of His mind. How could it be!

But the great purpose and passion of His life stands out most sharply in the words of His last imperial command. He shows the whole of His heart in that stirring "Go ye *into all the world* and make disciples of *all the nations.*" The gospel is to be preached to *the whole creation.* The passion of Jesus' heart was to change the world by winning the world. And that passion has grown more intense in waiting. With Him everything else bends to that passion. Nothing less will satisfy His heart.

2

The Master's Plan

Will the World Be Won?

The great passion of God's heart is a love-passion. Love never fails. It waits and, if need be, waits long; but it never fails to get what it is waiting for. Love sacrifices, though it never uses that word. It does not know it *is* sacrificing, it is so absorbed in its gripping purpose. There may be keen-cutting pain, but it is clean forgotten in the passion that burns within. God means to win His world of men back home to Himself.

But some earnest friend is thinking of an objection to all this talk about a world being won. True, you are taken all anew with the great picture of God's passion of love in the opening page of the Bible. But all the time we have been talking together you have been having a cross cutting train of thought underneath. It has been saying, "Isn't this going a bit too far? will the whole world be won?"

Let us talk about that for a while. All our lives we have been used to hearing about *soul-winning*. We have been urged, more or less, to do it. A favorite motto in some Christian workers' conventions has been, "Win one." But this idea of winning the world has not been preached. At first it does not seem exactly orthodox.

The old-time preaching, of which not so much is heard now, except in restricted quarters, is that the whole world is lost, and that we are to save people out of it. We used to be told that the world is bad, and only bad—bad beyond redemption, and doomed. In his earlier years Dwight L. Moody used to say often with his great earnestness that this is a doomed world, and that the great business of life is to save men out of it.

But of late years there has been a distinct swing away from this sort of preaching and talking. Everything we humans do seems to go by a pendulum swing: first one side, then the other. Now we hear a very different sort of preaching. This is really a good world. There is some wickedness in it, to be sure. Indeed, there is quite a great deal of it. But in the main it is not a bad world, we are told.

The old-time preaching was chiefly concerned with getting ready for heaven. Now preaching is concerned, for the most part, with living pure, true lives right here on the earth. And that change is surely a good one. But it is also the common thing to be told that the world is not nearly so bad as we have been led to believe.

Some Bad Drifts

It is striking that with the change in preaching emphasis has come a change of talk about sin, the thing that was supposed to be responsible for making the world so bad. Sin is not such a damnable thing now, apparently. It is largely constitutional weakness, or prenatal predilection, or the idiosyncrasy of individuality. (Big words are in favor here. They always make such talk seem wise and plausible.) Heaven has slipped largely out of view, and hell even more so. Churchmen in the flush of phenomenal material prosperity, with full stomachs and luxurious homes and pews, are well content with things as they are in this present world, and do not propose to move.

And with that it is easy to believe what we are freely told, that there is really no need of giving our Christian religion to the heathen world. Those peoples have religions of their own that are remarkably good. At least, they are satisfactory to them. Why disturb them? They are doing very well. This talk about their being lost, and needing a Savior, is reckoned out of date. The old common statements about so many thousands dying daily, and going out into a lost eternity, are not liked. They are called lurid. And, indeed, they are not used nearly so much now as once.

This swing has had a great influence upon the mass of church members, and upon their whole thought of the work of world evangelism in general. There is a vaguely expressed, but distinctly felt idea both in the church and outside of it (for the two seem to overlap as never before) that the sending of missionaries and Christian workers is really not to save peoples from being lost. That sort of talk is almost vulgar now.

Missionary evangelism is really a sort of good-natured neighborliness. It is benevolent humanitarianism in which we may all help, more or less (usually less), regardless of our beliefs or lack of beliefs, our church membership or attendance. We should show these heathen our improved methods of living. We have worked out better plans of housekeeping and schooling, of teaching and doctoring, and farming and all the rest of it. And now we want to help those poor deficient peoples across the seas.

We think we are a superior people in ourselves, as well as in our type of civilization, decidedly so. And having taken good care of ourselves, and laid up a good snug sum, we can easily afford to help those backward faraway neighbors a bit. It is really the humanitarian thing to do.

Such seems to be the general drift of much of the present-day talk about world evangelism. The church, and its members individually, have grown so rich that they have forgotten that they were ever poor. The table is so loaded with dainties that they are quite willing to be generous with the crumbs, even cake crumbs.

Great Incidental Blessings

Now, without doubt the sending of the missionaries has vastly improved conditions of human life in the foreign mission lands. The missionaries have been the forerunners of great improvements. They have been the pioneers blazing out the paths along which both trade and diplomacy have gone with the newer and better civilization of the West. Civilization has developed marvelously in the Western half of the world. And the missionaries have been its advance agents into the stagnant East, and the savage wilds of the Southern Hemisphere.

Full, accurate knowledge of nature's resources and laws, and adaptation of that knowledge to practical uses, have been among the most marked conditions of the Western world during the past century. And, as a result, education, medical and hygienic and sanitary science, and development of the earth's soil (and resources above and below the soil) have gone forward by immense strides. So far as is known, our progress in such matters exceeds all previous achievements in the history of the race.

And some of all this has been seeping into the heathen world. It has not gotten in far yet—only into the topsoil, and about the edges, so far. The progress in this regard has seemed both rapid and slow. When we consider that the great mass of these peoples have not yet gotten even a whiff of the purer, better civilization of the Western nations, the progress seems slow. But when we remember the incalculably tremendous inertia, and the strangely stagnant spirit of heathen lands, it seems rapid.

The effort to get the unevangelized nations simply to clean up, to open the windows and let in some fresh air, and use plain soap and water to scrub off the actual dirt, makes one think of the typical small boy's dislike of being washed. It has been a hard job. Yet a great beginning has been made. The boy seems to be beginning to find out that his face *is* dirty, and *feels* dirty. And that is an enormous gain.

The World Really Lost

Yet while this is good, and only good, it is not the thing we are driving at in missions. While it would fully warrant all the expenditures of money, and vastly more than has yet been given, it should be said in clearest, most ringing tones that all this is *merely incidental*. It is blessed. It is sure to come. And remarkably, it always has come where the gospel of Jesus is preached.

Yet this is not the thing aimed at in missions. The one driving purpose is to carry to men *a Savior from sin*. And to take Him so earnestly and winsomely that men yonder shall be wooed and won to the real God, whom they have lost knowledge of.

It cannot be said too plainly that the world *is*

lost. It has strayed so far away from the Father's house that it has lost all its bearings, and cannot find its way back without help. The old preaching that this is a lost world is true.

But we need to remember the different uses of that word *world*. In the old-time conception it was used in a loose way as meaning the spirit that actuates men. The scheme of selfishness and wickedness and sinfulness which has overcast all life is commonly spoken of in the Bible as the world spirit. In that sense the world is bad, and only bad. Men are to be saved out of it, as Moody said.

But in the other, more prevalent use, that word *world* simply means the whole race of men. And we must remind ourselves vigorously of the plain truth that this is a lost world. That is to say, men have gotten away from God. They completely misunderstand Him. Then they do more, and worse—they misrepresent and slander Him. The result is complete lack of trust in Him. They have lost their moorings, and have drifted out to deep sea with no compass on board. Thick fogs have risen and shut out sun and stars and every guiding thing. They are hopelessly and helplessly lost, and need someone to bring the compass so as to get back to shore, back home to God.

But this world of men is to be changed—won back to God. Jesus said He came to save the world. And He will not fail nor rest content until this has become a saved world. He said that He gave His life for the life of the world. And the world in its own heart will yet know the fulness of His throbbing passion.

This does not mean that all men will be saved. There seems to be clear evidence in the Book that some will insist on preferring their own way to God's. And I am sure I do not know anything except what the Book teaches. It is the only reliable source of information I have been able to find so far. It must be the standard, because it is the standard.

There will be a group of stubborn irreconcilables holding out against all of God's tender pleading. While on Patmos John saw a vision of glory, with a marvelous beauty and sweep, but it also had a lake of fire and a group of men insisting upon going their own way. If a man choose that way, he may. He is still in the likeness of God in choosing to leave out God. He remains a sovereign in his own will, even in the hell of his own choosing.

God's Method of Saving

The method of saving is by *winning*. The Father would not be content with anything else. Such a thing as might be represented by throwing a blanket over the head of a horse in a burning stable, and so getting it out by coaxing, and forcing, and hiding the danger, is not to be thought of here. Sin is never smoothed over by God, nor its results, their badness and their certainty.

He would have us see the sin as ugly and damning as it actually is, and see Him as pure and holy and winsome as He is; and then He would have us reject the sin and choose Himself. The method of much modern charity, the long-range charity that helps by organization, without the personal relation and warm touch, is unknown to God. He touches every man directly with His own warm heart, and appeals to him at closest quarters.

Man's highest power is his power of choosing. It is in choosing that he is most like God. God's plan is to clear away the clouds, sweep down the cobwebs that bother our eyes so, and let us get such a look at Himself that we will be caught with the sight of His great face, and choose to come, and to come a-running back to Himself. The world will be saved by its own choosing to be saved. It will be saved by being won. Men will choose to leave sin and accept God's Savior, Jesus Christ.

This is a great method. It is the only method God could use. The creative love-passion of His heart is that we should choose Him in preference to all else, and choose life with Him up on His level as the only life.

And the method of winning is by getting each man's consent. The old cry of soul-winning is the true cry. It tells the method of work for us to follow. Each man is to be won by his own free glad consent. The method is to be one by one; and the results, a great multitude beyond the power of any arithmetic to count. Soul-winning is the method, and world-winning is the object and the final result.

The Program of World Evangelism

There is a program of world-winning repeatedly outlined in the Bible. That program has not always been clearly understood. Indeed, it may be said that for the most part it has been misunderstood, and still is by many. And, as a result, many churchmen have lost their bearings, and strayed far from the Master's plan for their own lives and service. It helps greatly to get the program clearly in mind, so we can steer a straight course, and not get confused or lost.

The first item of that program is *worldwide evangelization*. That is the great service and privilege committed to the church, and to every Christian, for this present time. *Every other service is second to this*. This does not mean worldwide conversion. That comes later. It does mean a full, winsome sharing of the story of Jesus' gospel, to all nations and to all men.

It means the sharing of the gospel by all sorts of helpful, sensible means, especially the printed page, and the practical helping of men in every way that they can be helped. Above all, it means the warm, sympathetic, brotherly touch. Not simply by preaching; that surely, but in addition to that the practical preaching of the gospel by all possible means.

When that has been accomplished, the kingdom will come. The King will come, and with Him the kingdom. There will be radical changes in all the moral conditions of the earth. The world will then seem to be indeed a changed world.

There will be many who have simply been swung into line outwardly by the general movement among the mass of peoples, just as is always the case. But our King wants wholehearted love and service.

And so, at the end of the kingdom period, there will come another crisis. It is spoken of by John in his Revelation vision (20:7, 8) as a loosing of Satan, and a renewal of his activity among men. That used to puzzle me. I wondered why, when that foul fiend has once been securely fastened up, he should be loosed again. But I am satisfied that the reason is that at the end of the kingdom time there is to be full opportunity for those who are not at heart loyal to Jesus, and who simply bow to Him because the crowd is doing so, to be perfectly free to do and go as they choose.

Jesus wants a *heart* allegiance, and only that. The great thing is that every man will freely choose as he really prefers. This choice will both make and reveal character. And so there will be a final crisis. All who at heart prefer to do so may swing away from Jesus.

That crisis ends with the final and overwhelming defeat of Satan and all the forces of evil. He goes to his own place, the place he has chosen and made for himself; and all who prefer to leave God out will go by the moral gravitation of their own choice to that place with him.

Then follows the full vision of a changed world, which John pictures in such glowing colors in the last two chapters of Revelation, as a city come down from God out of heaven.

Early Moorings

There are two leading passages that speak of the program of world evangelism. You remember that during the last week of His life Jesus told His disciples of the fall of Jerusalem. They came earnestly asking for fuller information regarding the future events. They asked when the present period of time would come to an end. And in answering He said—and the answer became a pivotal passage around which much else swings—that the gospel of the kingdom would be preached in the whole inhabited earth for a testimony unto all nations. And then the end of the present age or period of time would come (Matt. 24:14).

The first council of the Christian church was held as a result of the remarkable success attending the beginning of worldwide evangelization. It was held in Jerusalem to consider the serious question of what to do with the great multitude of foreign or Gentile converts.

The church had been practically a Jewish church. But Paul had commenced his remarkable series of worldwide preaching tours. Great numbers of the outside peoples had accepted Christ, and been organized into Christian churches. Some of the Jewish church in Jerusalem thought that all of these should become Jewish in their observance of the old Mosaic requirements. Both Paul and Peter, the two great church leaders, objected to this.

It was at the close of the conference that James, who was presiding, outlined in his decision the program of world evangelism of which we have been talking together (Acts 15:13-18). He quoted from the prophecy of Amos. He said there were to be three steps or stages in working out God's plan.

First of all is the sharing of the gospel of Jesus with all the nations, in which work Paul had been so earnestly engaged, and the remarkable success of which it was that had given rise to the whole discussion. When this has been completed, the kingdom is to be established with the nation of Israel in the central place, the tabernacle of David set up. The purpose of this is that all the rest of the peoples on the earth, all the nations, "may *seek* after the Lord."

The purpose of the kingdom is the same, in the main, as is now the purpose of the church. It is to push forward on broader lines, and more vigorously than ever, the work of bringing all men back to the Father's house.

Other passages might be referred to, but these will answer our purpose just now. There is to be a changed world, and the Bible outlines plainly just how and when it will be won.

Service Unites

Now, I know that all ministers and Christian teachers are not agreed about this. There has been a controversy in the church, both long and sometimes bitter, unfortunately, about the Lord's return and the setting up of the kingdom. I have no desire to take any part in that, but instead, a strong desire to keep out of it. There is too much pressing emergency among men for helpful service to spend any time or strength in controversy.

In a word, it may be put this way. There are those who believe that Jesus' coming is a thing to be expected as likely to occur at any time, or within our lifetime, within any generation. His coming is to be the beginning of the kingdom period, when all peoples will be loyal to Him.

The others believe that the preaching of the gospel will bring the whole world into allegiance, and that will be the kingdom, and then Jesus will return. Both agree fully that the thing to be desired, and which will come, is the worldwide acknowledgment of Jesus as Savior and King.

It may be added, however, that in later years there has been a third great group in the church, which is really the largest of the three. These people practically ignore the teaching about an actual return of Jesus to the earth. They believe that He has already come, and is continually coming in the higher ideals, the better standards, and nobler spirit that pervade society.

If it be true that the present preaching of the gospel is to result in winning the whole world at once, without waiting for this program of which I have spoken, then there is in that a very strong argument for worldwide evangelization. For only so can the desired result be secured. And so we can heartily join hands together in service regardless of what we believe on this question. I make a rule not to ask a man on which side of the question he stands, but to work with him hand in hand so far as I can in spreading the glad good news of Jesus everywhere.

The difference of view regarding the Lord's return need not affect the practical working together of all earnest men. We are perfectly agreed that the great thing is to have the story of Jesus' dying and rising told out earnestly and lovingly to all men. And we can go at that with greatest heartiness, side by side.

The great concern now is to make Jesus fully known to all mankind. That is the plan. It is a simple plan. Men who have been changed are to be world-changers. Nobody else can be. The warm enthusiasm of grateful love must burn in the heart and drive all the life. There must be simple, but thorough organization.

The campaign should be mapped out as thoroughly as a presidential campaign is organized in America. The purpose of a presidential campaign is really stupendous in its object and sweep. It is to influence quickly, up to the point of decisive action, the individual opinion of millions of men, spread over millions of square miles, and that, too, in the face of a vigorous opposing campaign to influence them the other way. The whole country is mapped out and organized on broad lines and into the smallest details.

Strong, intelligent men give themselves wholly to the task, and spend tens of millions of dollars within a few months. And then, four years later, they proceed as enthusiastically as before to go over the whole ground again. We need as thorough organizing, as aggressive enthusiasm, and as intelligent planning for this great task which our Master has put into our hands.

And we have a driving motive greater than any campaign manager ever had or has—*a Jesus* who sets fire to one's whole being, with a passion of love that burns up every other flame. We need a church as thoroughly organized, and every man in it with a burning heart for this great service.

The World-Changing Climb

An old schoolmaster, talking to his class one morning, many years ago, told a story of an early experience he had had in Europe. He was one of a party traveling in France. They had gotten as far as Chamonix, and were planning to climb Mont Blanc. That peak, you know, is the highest of the Alps, and is called the monarch of European mountains. While it is now ascended every day in season, the climb is a very difficult task. It requires strength and courage and much special preparation, and is still attended with such danger that the authorities of Chamonix have laid down rigid regulations for those who attempt it. One's outfit must be reduced to the very lowest limit. And, of course, nothing else can be done while climbing. It absorbs all one's strength and thought.

There were two parties in the little square of the town, making their preparations with the guides. One young Englishman disregarded all the directions of the guides. He loaded himself with things which he positively declared were absolutely essential to his plans.

He had a small case of wine and some delicacies for his appetite. He had a camera with which he proposed to take pictures of himself and his party at different stages of the climb. He had a batch of notebooks in which he intended recording his impressions as he proceeded, which were afterward to be printed for the information, and, he hoped, admiration of the world. A picturesque cap and a gaily colored blanket were part of his outfit.

The old toughened guides, experienced by many a severe tug and storm for the difficulties ahead, protested earnestly. But they made no impression on the ambitious youth. At last they whispered together, and allowed him to have his own way. And the first party started.

Six hours later the second party followed. At the little inn where they spent the first night they found the wine and food delicacies. The guides laughed. "The Englishman has found that he cannot humor his stomach if he would climb Mont Blanc," one of them said grimly. A little farther up they found the notebooks and camera; still higher up, the colorful blanket and fancy cap had been abandoned. And at last they found the young fellow in leather jacket at the summit, exhausted and panting for breath.

He had encountered heavy storms, and reached the top of the famous mountain only at the risk of his life. But he had reached it. He had the real stuff in him, after all. Yet everything not absolutely essential had to be sacrificed. And his ideas of the meaning of that word *essential* had undergone radical changes as he labored up the steep.

Then the old teacher telling the story suddenly leaned over his desk and, looking earnestly at the class, said, "When I was young I planned out my life just as he planned out his climb. Food and clothing, and full records of my experiences for the world's information, were important components of my plan. But at forty I cared only for such clothes as kept me warm, and at fifty only for such food as kept me strong. And so steep was the climb up to the top I had set my heart upon that at sixty I cared little for the opinions of people, if only I might reach the top. And when I do reach it I shall not care whether the world has a record of it or not. The record is in safety above."

We laugh at the ambitious young Englishman. But will you kindly let me say, plainly, without meaning to be critical in an unkind sense, that *most of us do just as he did*. And will you listen softly, while I say this—many of us, when we find we cannot reach the top with our loads, let the top go, and pitch our tents in the plain, and settle down with our small plans and accessories. The plain seems to be quite full of tents.

The plan of the guides is *the plan* for the life-climb. That was Jesus' plan. He left behind and threw away everything that hindered, and at the last threw away life itself, that the world might find life. We must follow Him.

3

The Urgent Need

The Tender Heart

The human heart is tender. It answers quickly to the cry of need. But it is oftentimes hard to find. In Christian lands it is covered up with selfishness. And in unevangelized lands the selfishness seems so thickly crusted that it is hard to awaken even common humanitarian feeling.

But that heart once dug out, and touched, never fails to respond to the cry of need. We know how the cry raised in time of physical distress, some great disaster, or hunger will be listened to, and how quickly all men respond. When the terrible earthquake laid San Francisco in burning ruins, the whole nation stopped, gave a great heart throb, and then commenced at once sending relief. Corporations that are rated soulless and men that are spoken of as money-mad, knocking each other pitilessly aside in their greed for gold and power, all alike sent quick and generous help of every sort.

Besides expressing their sympathy in kindest and keenest word, they gave millions of dollars. Yet this might seem to be a family affair, as indeed it was. But the great famines in India and in other foreign lands farthest removed from us have awakened a like response in our hearts. Great sums have been given in money and supplies to feed the hunger of faraway peoples and help them sow their fields and get a fresh start.

There is a need far deeper and greater than that of physical suffering. That need is to know God, whom to know is to enter into fulness of life, both physical and mental, and into that life of the spirit that is higher and sweeter than either the physical or mental life. There is also a heart far more tender than the best which man of himself can offer. That tender heart is the human heart touched by the warm heart of God.

Many of us Christian people have had unusual blessing in having our hearts transported into real life by the touch of God. And there's much more of the same sort waiting our fuller touch with Him. And now we want to reach out to the needs of God's great world family, which is our own family because it is God's. We shall respond to it as freely and quickly and intelligently as He Himself did and does.

A Searching World

The whole of humanity seeks the joy and knowledge of our Lord. The very heathen religions themselves are the crying out, in the night, of men's hearts, after something they have not, and yet need so much. Strange things these pagan superstitions and monstrous practices and beliefs called religions! It has been rather the thing of late to speak somewhat respectfully of them, and rather apologetically. They have even been praised, so strangely do things get mixed up in this world of ours. It has been supposed that God was revealing Himself in these religions, and that in them men were reaching up to God, and *could* reach up to Him through them.

Heathen religions really are the twilight remnants of the clear direct light of God that once lightened all men; *but* this light has been so mixed through, and covered up with error and superstition and unnatural devilish lust, that these pagan beliefs are wholly inadequate to lead any man back home to God. In almost all of them there is indeed some distinct kernel of truth. But that kernel has been invariably shut up in a shell and bur that are hard beyond any power of cracking, to get at the kernel of truth for practical help, even if the people knew enough to try.

We hear of the pathetic groping of man's heart after God. But the groping is in the pitch dark, and amid a mass of foul, filthy cobwebs that blind eyes with their dust and grime all through life. I have no doubt that untold numbers of true hearts in heathen lands are feeling after God, and in some dim way coming into touch with

Him. He is not far from any one of them; but they find Him chiefly in spite of their religions, rather than through any help found in them.

The story is told of a Chinese tailor who had struggled hopelessly for light, and had finally found it in coming to know Jesus. He put his idea of the heathen religions that he knew, and had tried, in this simple vivid way:

"A man had fallen into a deep, dark pit, and lay in its miry bottom, groaning and utterly unable to move. He heard someone walking by close enough to see his plight. But with stately tread the other man walked on without volunteering to help. That is Mohammedanism.

"Confucius walking by approached the edge of the pit, and said, 'Poor fellow! I am sorry for you. Why were you such a fool as to get in there? Let me give you a piece of advice: If ever you get out, don't get in again.' That is Confucianism.

"A Buddhist priest next came by and said: 'Poor fellow! I am very much pained to see you there. I think if you could scramble up two-thirds of the way, or even half, I could reach you and lift you up the rest.' But the man in the pit was entirely helpless and unable to rise. That is Buddhism.

"Next the Savior came by, and, hearing the poor man's cries, went to the very brink of the pit, stretched down and laid hold of him, brought him up, and said, 'Go, and sin no more.' This is Christianity."

The awful, immoral conditions prevalent throughout the heathen world are the most graphic comment on the influence of those religions. It can be said that, instead of ever helping up to God and the light, they drag down to the devil and to black darkness. There is not only an utter lack of any moral uplift in them, but a deadly downward pull. The very things called religions point out piteously the terrible need of these peoples.

Now, what is it that these people need, and that we can give to them? May I first remind you what they do not need? Well, let it be said as plainly as it can be that they do not need the transferring to heathen soil of our Western church systems, nor our schemes of organizations. It is not our Western creeds and theology that they stand in need of.

Of course, there is need for both churches and organizations. Only so will the work be done, and what is gained held together. But these are in themselves temporary. They are immensely important and indispensable, but not the chief thing. The great need is *the story of Jesus*—the winsome telling, the tirelessly patient and persistently gentle sharing of the story of love, God's love as revealed in Jesus. We must tell of Jesus' promises to put a new moral power inside a man that will make him new.

Accustomed to the Night

The greatness of men's need stands out most pathetically in this, that men do not know their need. They have become so accustomed to the night that they do not care for the sunlight. They have been hungry so long that the sense of hunger and the call of appetite have wholly gone.

There is a simple, striking story told of two famous Scandinavians, Ole Bull, the great violinist, and John Ericsson, the great inventor, who taught the world to use the screw propeller in steam navigation. The former was a Norwegian, the latter a Swede. They had been friends in early life, but drifted apart and did not meet again until each had become famous. The old friendship was renewed on one of Ole Bull's tours to America.

As Bull was leaving his friend, after a delightful visit, he gave him a cordial invitation to attend his concert that evening. But the matter-of-fact, prosaic Ericsson declined, pleading pressure of work, and saying that he had no time to waste on music.

Bull renewed his invitation, time and again, finally saying, "If you won't come, I'll bring my violin down here to your shop and play." "If you do," replied the famous engineer laughingly, "I'll smash the thing to pieces." The violinist, knowing the marvelous, almost supernatural power of his instrument to touch and awaken the human heart into new life, felt curious to know what effect it would have on this scientific man steeped in his prosaic physics. So he planned a bit of strategy.

Taking the violin with him, Bull called upon

Ericsson at his workshop one day. He removed the strings and screws and apron, and called Ericsson's attention to certain defects, asking about the scientific and acoustic principles involved, and discussing the effects of the different grain of certain woods. From this he went on to a discussion of sound waves. Finally, to illustrate his questions, he put the parts back together, and bringing the bow softly down upon the tense strings, drew out a few marvelously sweet, rich tones.

At once the workmen in the shop dropped their tools and listened with wide-eyed wonder. Ole Bull played on and on, with his great skill, making the workshop a place of worship. When finally he paused, Ericsson lifted his bowed head, and showed eyes that were wet. Then he said softly, with a touch of reverent awe in his voice, "Play on! Don't stop. Play on. *I never knew before what it was that was lacking in my life.*"

That is what men everywhere say when they come to know Jesus. They fight against knowing Him because of their ignorance of Him. At home, prejudice against theology of this sort and that, against some preaching, or church service, or some Christian people they have unpleasant memories of perhaps, bars the way. Abroad, prejudice against their treatment at the hands of Christian nations, or against anything new, shuts the door with a slam and a sharp push of the bolt.

It takes great diplomacy, love's diplomacy, the

combination of serpent and dove, subtlety and harmlessness, to get an entrance. But when the door is pried open, or coaxed open enough for some sound or sight of Jesus to get in, men passionately cry out, "This is what I need. This Jesus is the thing lacking in my life!"

4

The Pressing Emergency

The October Panic

Some years ago a man walked up the steps of a well-known bank in lower New York, about a half hour before opening time, and stood before the shut door. In a few minutes another came, and stood waiting beside him. Others came, one by one, until soon a small group stood in line, waiting for the door to open.

A messenger boy, coming down the street, quickly took in the unusual sight. He was not old enough to have been through any of New York's notable panics, and he had never witnessed a run on a bank; but quick as a flash, or as a Wall Street messenger boy, he knew by instinct that a run was on at that bank. Instantly he started running down the street to tell others.

No prairie wild fire ever spread so quickly as the news ran over phone lines of the beginning of that run. As though by some sort of invisible force, the news seemed to spread through the financial district. Every bank president seemed to know at once. Then it spread throughout the city, and into the suburbs.

So began what has been called the October panic, which quickly spread through the land, and then throughout the world until every bank, and every capital city abroad, felt the sharp tightening of the pocketbook.

It was a strange panic. You could not tell just what was responsible for it. The very variety of explanations, editorial and other, told of the lack of a common understanding of what caused it. There had been no famine or drought. The crops, the chief financial barometer of the country's condition, had been remarkably abundant. There had been no overproduction or glutting in the industrial world. Indeed, great numbers of concerns had been embarrassed by orders that they could not fill fast enough. The cause seemed to be wholly in people's *minds*. A spirit of distrust of some of the economic leaders and of their methods was abroad. That feeling of fear sent a few men, by an unplanned concert of action, to a certain bank before ten o'clock one morning.

The unusual sight of a few men, standing in line waiting for the opening of that bank door was like a lighted match to a barn full of dry hay. At the first inkling of a suggestion of a financial panic money began to disappear. Nothing is so cowardly in its cautiousness as money. Scholarship comes next to it. The savings of years are very tightly gripped by most human hands. As though by magic, money began hunting dark holes in stockings and cellars and safety-deposit boxes. And the hard grip of the panic was quickly felt everywhere. It was a panic brought on by fear. A terrible danger was at hand.

At once the regular habit of life was disturbed for great numbers of men. The Secretary of the Treasury left his Washington desk and spent several days in New York so as to be able to give the help of the government's funds and enormous prestige where they would count for most, and to give it promptly. Bank officials and other financial leaders cut social engagements and everything else that could be cut, and devoted themselves to meeting the sudden emergency. They ate scantily, both to save time and for lack of appetite, and to help keep their heads clear for quick decisive thinking and action. The tension was intense. Men sat up all night conferring on what would be the best measures to take.

A group of the leading moneymen met in the private quarters of one of their numbers, about whose rugged personality and leadership they instinctively rallied. More than one night the grey dawning light of the morning found them, with white, drawn faces, still in conference. The emergency gripped them. And emergency always does. The habits of life are upset, helter-skelter, in the effort to avert the threatening danger. That was an emergency in the money world. Grave danger threatened. Everything else was forgotten, and every bit of available resource strained to turn the danger aside. It *was* turned aside. That was a splendid achievement. And even though men have been feeling the effects for this whole year, what they have felt is as nothing compared with what might have come.

Danger and Victory

An emergency means a great danger threatening; perhaps life itself is at stake. But it means, too, that if the danger can be gripped and overcome there will be great victory. Two possibilities come up close and stare each other angrily in the face; the possibility of great disaster impending, and of great victory over it within grasp, if there be a reaching hand to grasp it. The deciding thing is the human element, the strong, quick hand stretched out. If strength can be concentrated, the situation gripped, then great victory is assured. But it takes the utmost concentration of strength, with rare wisdom and quick, steady action, to avert the flood. If this is not done, either because of lack of relationship or of enough strength or interest, disaster comes.

Such emergencies come to us constantly. A severe illness lays its hand upon a loved one in the home. The crisis comes. Death and life stand in the sick room, eyeing each other. Either one may be victor. No one can tell surely which it will be. And every effort is strained, the habit of life broken, other matters forgotten and neglected, that death may be staved off, and life wooed to stay. And when the crisis passes safely, the joy over the new lease of life makes one forget all the cost of strain and effort.

Who of us cannot recall some time back there, when some emergency came in business matters, and personal and home expenses and plans were cut down to the lowest notch, to the bleeding point, that the emergency might be safely met?

Teachers and parents know that moral emergencies come at intervals in a child's life, until young manhood or womanhood is reached. One of the greatest tasks in child training is to note the emergency, and meet it successfully. And what keenness and patience and subtlety this involves only he knows who has been through the experience.

Spiritual Contests

Emergencies come in spiritual matters, too. They are the hardest kind to meet. It is hardest to make people see them and grip them. In the life of many a church a spiritual emergency has come, but has not been met. The church goes on holding services, raising money and paying it out, going through all the proper forms, but with the life itself quite gone out of it. The basic routine is being kept in motion by a humanly manipulated electric current.

Evangelistic leaders say that such emergencies come in their campaigning. There has to be a struggle of spiritual forces. And the victory that comes, comes only as a result of close hand-to-hand conflict of soul by the leaders.

We all know that such crises come in our personal experience. And those who know about changing things by prayer do not need to be told of the emergency that comes at times, nor of how it requires a tightening of all the buckles, a new reviewing of the promises on which prayer rests, a new steadying of one's faith, a quietly persistent hanging on, a more intense insistence of spirit in prayer and more "arrow-praying" in the daily round of work—sending out the softly breathed heart pleadings while busy with common duties, until the assurance comes that the danger is past and the victory secure.

It is remarkable to what an extent the great events of history have been emergency events. With the greatest reverence, it can be said that history's central event, the dying of Jesus, was an emergency action. Even though we understand clearly that it was known and counseled from before the foundation of the world, that He was to shed His precious blood for our salvation, His dying can never be fully understood save as a great emergency measure, *the* great emergency measure, because of the crisis made by sin.

Now that is the sort of thing—an emergency—that is now on in this great task of world evangelization which Jesus has committed to our hands. Some of you may be strongly inclined to lift your eyebrows and ask—Is there really any such emergency? I know that people do not like those words *crisis* and *emergency*. It is much more comfortable to think that things are going on very smoothly and well. Even though all is not just as we might choose to have it, yet we like to think that it will turn out well. There is a sort of optimism that is very popular. Things will all come out right somehow, we like to think. But the fact is that things do not turn out right of themselves. They have to be turned by somebody who gives heart and life to the task.

It can be said with sane, sober sense that without doubt there is an emergency, and a great one, in this matter of world evangelism. It is, of course, true that in a sense there is *a continual emergency* here. There are tens of thousands of our foreign brothers and sisters slipping the tether of life daily. The light might easily have been taken to them, and have changed their choices. But such has not been the case, and the dark shadow of the possibility of their separating themselves forever from God, through wrong choice persisted in, hangs down over each one of them. There can be no darker shadow except the actual knowledge that they have so separated themselves from life in Him.

The Current Crisis

But quite distinct from that, and in addition to it, it is quite safe to say that there is *an emer-*

gency now going on in a lost world such as it has never known before. Such is the mature judgment of Christian leaders of many other lands.

And we do well to remind ourselves that we have some remarkable men among those leaders. There are nationals on the foreign fields (and at the missionary helm) of the most remarkable ability and genius. There are today men of statesmanlike grasp and power, who could easily have taken front rank in public life, in diplomacy, and professional life, men fully able to fill the presidential chair and do so masterfully, who are giving their lifeblood to the task of world evangelism.

The sober judgment of these men, taken from every angle of vision, is that the present is a time of unparalleled emergency. It exists peculiarly in Communist and Arab/Moslem lands. It has been caused by a number of things that now come together with such force as to make a crisis, *the* crisis of missions, the gravest that has yet come, and that, it is probably safe to say, will ever come. For the future will be largely settled, one way or the other, within a few years.

At the basis of all is *the great need,* of course. That looms big and gaunt and spectral in any survey of the matter.

Then *the neglect* by the church for many generations has greatly intensified the present situation. The Master's plan plainly is that every generation of the church shall give the gospel to its contemporaries; *that is, to all the people living in the world at that time.* Every generation of men must have the gospel afresh.

A Westernized Heathenism

Now, let us look briefly at this present pressing emergency. There are grave perils threatening, and a great victory is possible.

Well, first of all there is real danger of *a new aggressive heathenism*—a new, energetic, but distinctly un-Christian civilization in the heathen world. Many thoughtful men who are keenly watching the world movement believe that without doubt there is to be a new leadership of the human race in the Orient. It *may* be a heathen leadership.[1] That danger is a distinct possibility. The new world-leadership may have all the enormous energy and mental keenness of Christian peoples, but without the Christian spirit.

That means practically a new heathenism, no longer asleep, but wide awake; no longer being manipulated by the Western nations, but maybe manipulating and managing them. An aroused, organized, energized heathen world, with all the science and inventiveness and restless aggres-

[1]Little did S. D. Gordon realize when writing these words at the turn of the century that within four decades all of China, and several other Oriental nations, would fall into the grasp of Communism. In fact, S. D. Gordon penned this prophecy five years before the Communist revolution was launched in Russia.

siveness of the Western nations *and,* mark you, all the spirit of the old, godless, Christless heathenism dominating its new life—that is the danger.

The heathen world is awake at last after a sleep of centuries. It is sitting up, rubbing its eyes, and taking notice. It is entering upon a cloudless morning. What that life shall be depends entirely on the church's waking up. That means, to be more practical, that it depends on your and my waking up, just now, and doing what we easily can. We must be alert to the possibility of a new life of energized, Westernized heathenism! It may get merely our energy and mental awakeness without the Christian spirit that gave these qualities to us.

These two opposite things are standing by the bedside and eyeing each other. Which will get the patient? Who knows? If the church fail! This is a real peril seriously threatening. It is probably far more grave and far more likely than the best-informed and keenest observer is aware of.

A Powerless Christianity

Then there is a second danger climbing in fast on the heels of this, a danger that is already being plainly felt. *These peoples may turn away from a Christianity that seems powerless to them.* As they come to know better the simple principles of our faith, they may see that we are not true to it. Our Master bade us go everywhere and tell all men of Him, and tell them most and best by the way we live. *But we have not done it.* The church of the past nineteen centuries, taken as whole, has not done it. The church today, taken as a whole, is not doing it.

How many times have the missionaries or Christian nationals been obliged to listen to the question, which is a reproach rather than a question, "Why didn't you come before? My father loved and died in distress, seeking for this light you bring us now. *Why didn't your father come and tell my father?*" If they find that our faith has not changed *us* enough to master our lives, they will naturally doubt if, after all, there is any more real practical power in it than in their own heathen beliefs.

Christianity *seems* better in theory, but it apparently loses its ideals in the stiff test of practice. Foreign peoples would be wrong in thinking that, of course. But what conclusion is more natural to the crowd that never thinks deeply? When difficulties and hardships come in the way of their acceptance of Christ, and the easiest course is not to, how easy to throw the whole thing aside!

Death or Deep Water

If it be true that every generation *needs* the gospel, it is just as true that every generation of Christians *needs to give* the gospel. It is the very life of a Christian to give himself out in earnest service for others. The man who is failing there has started on the downgrade in his Christian life. If we lose the spirit of "go," we have lost the very Christian spirit itself. *A disobedient church will become a dead church.* It will die of heart failure.

It was John's Angel with eyes of searching flame, and tongue of keen-edged sword, and feet that had been through the fire, who said to a Christian church, "I will move thy candlestick out of its place except thou change thy ways" (Rev. 2:5). The candlestick is not the light. It holds the light. The church's great mission is to be the world's light-holder.

But snuffed-out candles and cobwebby windowpanes seem to have been in evidence sometimes. The Christian church in some lands has plainly lost its privilege of service, and lost its life too. Old dead programs are kept up, but all life has gone.

Long years ago, in the days before steam navigation, an ocean vessel came from a long sea voyage, up St. George's Channel, headed for Liverpool. When the pilot was taken on board, he cried abruptly to the captain, "What do you mean? You've let her drift off toward the Welsh coast, toward the shallows. Muster the crew." The crew was quickly mustered, and the pilot told the danger in a few short words, and then said sharply, "Boys, it's death or deep water: hoist the mainsail." And only by dint of hardest work was the ship saved.

If I could get the ear of the church today I would, as a great kindness to it, cry out with all the earnestness of soul I could command, "*It's death or deep water:* deep water in this holy service of changing the world or death from foundering."

Saved by Saving

And then there is yet a graver peril threatening. There is serious danger of a *heathenized Christanity* dominating our boasted Christian civilization and Christian lands.

That is to say, there may be the energy and keen mental life without the mellowing and sweetening influence of the Christian spirit. The restless aggressiveness may come without the poise, the ceaseless activity without the deeper steadying quality, the keenness without the softening touch of the true life. In other words, if we do not evangelize the lost, they will exert an influence on us that will practically amount to their draining power from the church.

Already such influences are seeping in at more than one crack. Heathen wedges are slipping their thin edges in, in our land. They will become more and more extensive, in time influencing our whole moral fabric, and affecting our whole national life.

During some recent researches among the ruins of Pompeii the explorers turned up a find that told its own story. It was the body of a crippled boy. He was lame in his foot. And around the body there was a woman's arm, a finely shaped, beautiful, bejeweled arm. The mute find told its simple story. The great stream of fire suddenly coming from the volcano, the crowd fleeing for life, the little cripple unable to get along fast enough, the woman's heart touched, her arm thrown about the boy to aid his escape; then the overtaking fire flood, and both lost. The arm that was stretched out to save another was preserved, and only that. All the rest of the brave would-be rescuer's body had gone. The saving part was saved. Only that mercifully outstretched to save another was itself saved.

The church or the man that selfishly saves his life shall lose it. He that forgets about his own life in eagerly saving others shall find that he has saved his own life, and that it has grown into a new fulness and richness.

There are some dark, ugly faces peering into ours. But there is another face among them. It is a very bright face, with eyes all aglow, and features all shining with light. It is the face of victory over every danger and difficulty that threaten. Many believe that the emergency will be met. The victory will surely be achieved. But the fact to mark keenly, just now, is that it will be achieved only by a vigorous, masterful gripping of the present pressing emergency.

Ah God! may Thy church—we men and women who make up Thy church, who *are* Thy church—may we see the emergency, and be gripped by it for Jesus' sake; aye, for mankind's sake; for the church's sake; for our own sake. In Jesus' great name.

5

The Past Failure

God's Failures

As amazing as it sounds, God's plans sometimes seem to fail. That is to say, the plan He has made and set His heart upon fails. Now before you form an opinion concerning the theological soundness in these words, please read on.

Eden was God's plan for man. A weedless, thornless world garden of great beauty and fruitfulness; a man and woman living together in sweet purity and strong self-mastery; their children growing up in such an atmosphere, trained for the highest and best; the earth with all its wondrous forces developed and mastered by man; full comradeship and partnership between man and all the living creation, beast and bird; and in the midst of all God Himself walking and working in closest touch with man in all his enterprises—that was God's plan for man. But it failed.

The plan for Israel was a failure, too. The main

purpose of Israel's being made God's peculiar people has failed up to the present hour. That plan originally was a simple shepherd people, living on the soil, close to nature. They were to be, not a democracy ruled by the direct vote of the people in all things; nor a republic ruled by the vote of selected representatives; nor yet a kingdom ruled over by the will of an autocrat; but something quite distinct from all of these, what men have been pleased to call a theocracy.

That is to say, God Himself was to be their ruler in a very real, practical sense, directing and assisting them in the working out of all their national life. They were to combine all the best in each of the above-mentioned forms of government, with a something added, a something not in any hitherto known form of government. They were to be wholly unlike the other nations, utterly unambitious politically, neither exciting war upon themselves by others nor ever making war upon others. Their great mission was to be a teacher-nation to all the earth, teaching the great spiritual truths, and, better yet, embodying these truths in their personal and national life.

But the plan failed. The glitter of the other nations turned them aside from God's plan. They set up a kingdom, "like all the nations," very much like them.

Then God worked with Israel where they would work with Him. He planned a great kingdom to overspread the earth in its rule and blessed influence, but not by the aggression of war and oppression. Their later literature is all aflood with the glory of the coming King and kingdom. Yet when the King came they rejected Him and then killed Him. They failed at the very point that was to have been their great achievement. God's plan failed. The Hebrew people from the point of view of the direct object of their creation as a nation have been a failure up to the present hour.

God's choice for their first king, Saul, was a failure, too. No man ever began life, nor king his rule, with better preparation and prospects. And no career ever ended in such dismal failure. God's plan for the man had failed.

Jesus' plan for Judas failed. The sharpest contrasts of possible good and actual bad came together in his career in the most startling way. He failed at the very point where he should have been strongest—his personal loyalty to his Chief.

There can be no doubt that Jesus picked Judas out for one of His inner circle because of his strong attractive traits. He had in him the making of a John, His intimate and the writer of the great Fourth Gospel. He might have been a Peter, rugged in his bold leadership of the early church. But, though coached and companioned with, loved and wooed, up to the very hour of the cowardly, contemptible betrayal, he failed to respond even to such influence as Jesus could exert. Jesus planned Judas the apostle. He became Judas the apostate, the traitor. He was to be a leader and teacher of the gospel. He became a miserable reproach and byword of execration to all men. Jesus' plan failed.

The Reproach of Failure

Will you please mark very keenly that *the failure always comes because of man's unwillingness to work with God?* It always takes two for God's plan—Himself and a man. All His working is through human partnership. In all His working among men He needs to work *with* men.

Some good earnest people do not like, and would not like, that blunt statement that God's plans sometimes fail. It seems to them to cast a reproach upon God. They may likely think it lacking in due reverence. But if these kind friends will sink the shaft of their thinking just a little deeper down into the mine of truth, they will find that the reproach is somewhere else.

There *is* reproach. Every failure that could have been prevented by honest work and earnest faithfulness spells reproach. And there is reproach here. But it is not upon God; it is upon man. *God's plan depends upon man.* It is always man's failure to do his simple part faithfully that causes God's plan to fail.

There is a false reverence that fears to speak plainly of God. It seeks by holding back some things, and speaking of others with very carefully thought out phrase, to bolster up God's side. True love has two marked traits: it is always plain-spoken in telling all the truth when it should be known, and it is always reverential. It cannot be otherwise. The bluntest words on the lips combine with the deepest reverence of spirit. God does not need to be defended. The plain truth need never be apologized for.

It is a false reverence that holds back some of the truth, lest stating it may seem to reflect on God's character. Such false reverence is a distinct hindrance. It holds back from us some of the truth, and the strong emphasis that the truth needs to arouse our attention and get into our sometimes thick heads. We men need the stirring up of plain truth, told in plainest speech. The church has suffered for lack of plain telling of the truth. The deepest, tenderest reverence insists upon plain talk, and reveals itself in such talk.

It is irreverent to hold back some of God's truth. For in this way men get wrong impressions of God. It is unfair as well as irreverent. Theology has sometimes been greatly taken up with adjusting its statements so as to defend God's character. But the plainest, fullest telling of truth is the greatest revealer of His great wisdom and purity and unfailing love.

God's Sovereignty

There has been a good deal of teaching about "God's sovereignty." Behind that mysterious, indefinite phrase has crept much that badly needs the clear, searching sunlight of day. God's sovereignty is commonly thought of as a sort of dead-weight force by which He compels things to come His way. If a man stand in the way of God's plan, so much the worse for the man. It is thought of as a sort of mighty army, marching down the road, in close ranks, with fixed bayonets. If you happen to be on that road, look out very sharply, or you may get crushed under foot.

I do not mean that the theologians put it in that blunt fashion, nor that I have ever heard any preacher phrase it in that way. I mean that as I have talked with the plain, common people, and listened to them, this is the distinct impression that comes continually of what God's sovereignty means to them. Then, too, the phrase has often been used, it is to be feared, as a religious cloak to cover up the shortcomings and shirkings of those who are not fitting into God's plan.

God *is* a sovereign. The truth of His sovereignty is one of the most gracious of all the truths in the blessed old Book of God. It means that the great gracious purpose and plan of God will finally be victorious. It means that in our personal lives He, with great patience and skill and power, works *through* the tangled network of circumstances and difficulties to answer our prayers, and to bring out the best results for us.

It means further that, with a diplomacy and patience only divine, He works *with* and *through* the intricate meshes of men's wills and contrary purposes to bring out good now—not good out of bad, that is impossible; but good in spite of the bad—and that finally all opposition will be overcome, or will have spent itself out in utter weakness, and so His purposes of love will be fully victorious.

But the practical thing to burn in deep just now is this, that *we can hinder God's plan.* His plans *have* been hindered, and delayed, and made to fail, because we would not work with Him.

And God *lets* his plan fail. This is a sign of His greatness. He will let a plan fail before He will be untrue to man's utter freedom of action. He will let a man wreck his career, that through the wreckage the man may see his own failure, and gladly turn to God. Many a hill is climbed only through a swamp road.

God cares more for a man than for a plan. The plan is only for the sake of the man. You say, "Of course." But, you know, many men think more of carrying through the plan on which they have set themselves, regardless of how it may hurt or crush someone in the way. God's plan is for man, and so it is allowed to fail, for the man's sake.

Yet, because the plan is always made for man's sake, it will be carried through, because by and by man will see it to be best. Many a man's character has been made only through the wrecking of his career. If God had had His way, He would have saved both life and soul, both the earthly career and the heavenly character.

Let us pause a moment to remember that God has carefully thought out a plan for every man, for each one of us. It is a plan for the *life,* these human years; not simply for getting us to what we may have thought of as a psalm-singing heaven, once we have been worn out down here.

God's plan is the best plan. For God is ambitious for us, more ambitious for you and me than we are for ourselves, though few of us really believe that. But He will carry out His plan—aye, He *can* carry it out only with our hearty consent. He must work *through* our wills. He honors us in that. With greatest reverence be it said that God waits reverently, hat in hand, outside the door of a man's will, until the man inside turns the knob and throws open the door for Him to come in and carry out His plan. *We can make God fail by not working with Him.* The greatest of all achievements of action is to find and fit into God's plan.

The Church's Mission

Now, God had and has a plan for His church. That plan is simply this: *the church was and is to be His messenger to the nations of the earth.* There are other matters of vast importance committed to the church, without doubt: the service of worship and the training and developing of the life of its members. But these, be it said very thoughtfully, are distinctly secondary to the service of taking the gospel to all men.

The chief and the secondary concerns of the

church are interwoven, each contributing to and dependent upon the other. But there is always a main purpose. And that here, without question, is the carrying of the message of Jesus fully to all the earth. In each generation the chief plan, to which all else was meant to be contributory, was that all men should hear fully and winsomely the great thrilling story of Jesus.

Shall I say that that plan has failed? It hurts too much even to repeat such words. I will not *say* the church has failed. But I will ask you to note God's plan for the church, and then in your inner heart to make your own honest answer.

And in making it remember the practical point is this—the church is *you*. *I* am the church. Its mission is mine. If I say it has failed, I am talking about myself. I can keep it from failing so far as part of it is concerned, the part that I am. My concern is not to be asking abstractly, theoretically, about the church, but about so much of it as I am.

In annual church reports, much space is given to telling of the *wealth* of the church. Of course, I suppose its wealth is meant to be an index of all its work. It may seem a bit odd to use the world's index finger to point out our faithfulness to our Master's will. It is used, of course, to impress the world in the way the world can most quickly and easily understand.

But the church was not meant by the Master to be a rich institution in money and property, though it has grown immensely so. The Master's thought was that its power and faithfulness should be revealed entirely in the extent to which all men of all nations know about Him and have been won to Him.

If we think only a little bit into the past history of the church, and then into present world conditions, we know the answer to that hurting question about the church's being a failure.

I know that many of you are thinking of the triumphs of the church, of her imperishable and incalculable influence upon the life of the world. And I will join you heartily in that, some other time. Just now we are not talking of that, but of just one particular fact of its history. One truth at a time makes sharper outlines and brings the whole circle of truth out more plainly.

I love to sing,

> I love Thy kingdom, Lord,
> The house of Thine abode,
> The Church our blest Redeemer saved
> With His own precious blood.

We shudder to think what past centuries would have been without the influence of the church.

But at present we are talking about something else. Let me ask you, softly: if God's plan for the church was that it was to be His messenger to all men, as you think back through nineteen centuries and then think about the moral conditions of the world today, would you say the plan had succeeded?

"Christ Also Waits"

There is some light here on that vexed question of the Lord's second coming, about which good, earnest people differ so radically. The Master said, you remember, that we were to be watching for His return. But many ask, how can we be watching when it is two thousand years since He told us to watch, and the event seems as far off as ever?

I remember one day in a Bible class the lesson was on the twelfth chapter of Luke, about watching for the Lord's return. Some of the class seemed to think that we should be in a constant attitude of expectancy, looking for His return. But one man, an earnest, godly old minister, asked, "How can you be looking expectantly for a *thousand years?*"

But will you mark keenly that *the teaching of Jesus Himself is that His return depends on His followers doing a certain thing* (Matt. 24:14)? When all men have been told fully of Jesus, then He will return and carry out a further part of His plan. Clearly, if the part we are to play has not been done, His part is delayed. The telling of all men about Jesus seems to bear a very close connection with what will occur when Jesus returns.

Some of our good friends have been much taken up with figuring out when the Lord will come back. Some of them seem to have great skill in making calendars. They even go so far as to fix exact dates. They seem to forget that word of the Master, "In such an hour as ye think *not* the Son of man cometh." If you think He will come at a certain given time, then you can know one thing certainly, that He will not come then.

The only calendar we men have is a calendar of *dates,* fitted to the movements of the sun and moon. God has a calendar, too, but it is a calendar of *events,* not of dates. The completion of His plans does not depend on so many revolutions of the earth about the sun, but on the faithful revolution of His followers in their movement around the earth, telling men of Jesus.

It looks very much as though the Master's coming has been delayed, and His plans delayed, because we have not done the preparatory part assigned us.

> The restless millions wait the light
> Whose coming maketh all things new.
> *Christ also waits*, but men are slow and late.
> Have we done what we could? Have I? Have you?

"Somebody Forgets"

A little fellow, of a very poor family, in the slum section of one of our large cities, was induced to attend a mission Sunday school. By and by, as a result of the teacher's faithful work, he became a Christian. He seemed quite bright and settled to his new Christian faith and life.

Someone, surely in a thoughtless mood, tried to test or shake his simple faith in God by a question. He was asked, "If God loves you, why doesn't He take better care of you? Why doesn't He tell someone to send you warm shoes and some coal and better food?"

The little fellow thought a moment, and then with big tears starting in his eyes, said, "I guess He does tell somebody, *but somebody forgets.*"

Without knowing it, the boy touched the sore point in the church's history. I wonder if it is the sore point with you or me.

6

The Coming Victory

Overcoming Failure

God's seeming failures are only for a while. To be sure, they are real. There is the tragic element in them. There is the deep, sad tinge of disappointment running throughout the Bible. Yet the failures are only for a time. Sometimes it seems a very long time, especially if you are living through some of it. But the time reaches eagerly to an end. Victory comes. And God's victory will be so great as to make us completely forget the failures that marred the road.

Eden was more than a plan. It was a prophecy of the final outcome. The Book of God begins with failure, but it ends with a glowing picture of great victory, painted with rose colors. Every feature of beauty and of good in Eden has grown greatly in the climax of John's Revelation. The garden of Genesis becomes a garden-city. All the simplicity and purity of garden life, and all the development and power represented by city life, are brought together. There is now a *river* of *life,* and the *tree* of life has grown into a grove.

And God is not through with that nation of Israel yet. The Jew cannot be lost. In every nation under heaven he can be found today, a walking reminder of God's plan. Every Jew, in whatever nation he may be found, is an unconscious prophecy of a coming fulfilment of God's purpose. The strange racial immortality of the Jew is a puzzle from every standpoint, except God's. He cannot be killed off, though men have never ceased trying to kill him off. The Jew looms up bigger today than he has for many generations.

The present strange, restless Jewish longing for national existence again, a longing that will not disappear, spells out the coming victory of God's plan after centuries of failure.[1] And even though the present tide may ebb, it will gather force for a new and fuller flood. When God's plan works out, the world will have a wholly new idea of national life, and of a world power without army or navy or any show of force, touching all men, and touching them only to bless.

Though King Saul failed, there was already the ruddy David, out among the sheep, waiting the anointing oil, and carrying about in his person the potential to become his nation's greatest king.

Judas failed to realize the promise of his earlier days. He struck the record note for baseness.

[1]Sadly, S. D. Gordon did not live to see Israel become a nation in May of 1948.

But Paul was being prepared by blood inheritance and scholarly training. Under the touch of the Master's own hand, he became the church's greatest leader in its life-mission. If Judas struck the lowest note, Paul rang the highest note of personal loyalty to Jesus and to His worldwide passion and purpose.

And the church has waked up. I said earlier, that if you look over the whole history of the church since its birthday on Pentecost, you are pained by the sore fact that the chief mission entrusted to it has been for the most part forgotten. There has been more forgetting of it, and neglecting it, than fulfilling it.

Yet always, be it keenly noted, in every generation of these centuries there have been those whose vision of Olivet never dimmed. There have always been those who have tried faithfully to carry out the church's great mission. The darkest days have never been without some of the brightest light, made all the brighter by the surrounding night.

"We Can Do It!"

But there is a new chapter of the church's life being written as we talk together. Its writing began in the closing twilight of the eighteenth century. That chapter is not finished yet. Some of its best pages are now being written, with more and better clearly coming.

Its first lines were written by a very common

pen. William Carey's English cobbler shop became a sounding board whose insistent, ringing messages began to waken the church. The church is waking up, and shaking itself, and tightening on its clothes, for the greatest work yet to be done in fulfilling the life-mission entrusted to it.

A hundred fifty years ago the fire of God found fresh kindling stuff in the hearts and brains of a few young college fellows in an old New England village. The sore need of the world crowded in upon them by night and by day. But they were few, and young, and unknown. And the task was stupendous. The rainstorm of a Sabbath afternoon drove them to the shelter of a haystack. And the storm of the world's need drove them to the shelter of prayer, and then to the shelter of a great purpose. With simple faith in God, and strong devotion to the great neglected task, they spoke out to the church the thrilling words, "We can do it if we will."

And on that same spot a hundred years later the church gathered. Those intense words had been heard. The church had awakened. Men with long service in faraway lands stood with those of the home circle. They talked of the past, but far more of the present and future. They revised the century-old motto. No group of scholars in the Jerusalem Chamber of Westminster Abbey ever did finer revision work. They said, "We can do it, *and* we will." No greater tribute to the memory of the faithful little haystack group was ever made than in that changed motto.

The young collegians' bold cry had sounded out throughout the church. And the church heard and roused up. The modern missionary movement is the most marked development of the past century of church history. It can be said that the church of our day in its missionary activity far exceeds the early church. That is to say, in certain particulars we have exceeded.

It is common to refer to the missionary zeal of the first centuries. Fresh from the Master's touch, the early church was chiefly a missionary church. One great purpose gripped it, and that was to take the news of Jesus everywhere. And they went everywhere. We know most about Paul's journeys in the Grecian and Roman worlds. But there is good evidence that there is another "Acts of Apostles" besides the one bound up in the Bible. Out to the farthest reaches of the earth they seem to have gone in those early days, preaching and winning men and establishing groups of practicing believers.

The *bulk* of the modern movement is without doubt greatly in excess of the early movement. The number of men out in various fields and the amount of money being given annually by the church in the free world are so much greater as to make comparison out of the question.

In the thoroughness of organization, the elements of permanency, the great variety of means used, the present probably exceeds by far the early movement. The statesmanlike study by church leaders of the whole world field, the steadiness of movement year after year, in spite of difficulties and discouragements, the careful, systematic effort to inform and arouse the home church—these are marked features of the present task of world evangelism. They are such as to awaken the deepest admiration of any thoughtful onlooker. In all of this the modern church is making a wholly new record.

Ahead, but Behind

Yet, while all this is true, it can be said just as truly that the church, *as a whole,* is so far behind the primitive church as, again, practically to leave comparison out of the question. The early Christians were so far ahead in the *mass* of their movement that we are scarcely in the lists at all. In the first century the *whole* church was an active missionary society. *Everyone* went and preached. The nearest approach to it in modern times probably is the movement of the Church of Korea. This Oriental people seems to have caught the early spirit. Our Korean brothers and sisters are taking their place as pacesetters for the church.

By contrast with the early church, the modern activity has been by a minority, really a small minority, though a steadily growing one. The leaders have struggled heroically against enormous odds in the backward pull of the majority.

Moreover, the early Christians went *everywhere*. That is, they went everywhere that they could, so far as open doors, or doors that could be pried open, let them. We have gone actually farther, and to more places probably, but we have not begun to get everywhere that we could.

Our ability to go, and the urgent requests for us to come, would carry us to thousands of places not yet touched. If we began to do things as the early church did, our efforts would stand out as one of the greatest movements in the history of the human race. If a small minority can make enormous strides, what could the whole of us do if we would!

A Minority Movement

Yet, be it keenly marked, these great strides have been made by a minority, who have followed strong leaders. The whole church is not yet awake. Many protest strenuously against being waked up. The alarm clocks bother them. Sometimes one is inclined to think that the foreign missionary boards are peculiarly placed between a refrigerator and a furnace.

Missionaries come back home fresh from the front fairly aflame with fervor of their enthusiasm. Their convictions of what could be done, and should be done, are apt to be spoken out with great positiveness. They seem to some to suggest in an uncomfortable way the thought of a glowing furnace. And many in the home churches seem able to listen with such indifference as to suggest to these returned men and women the chilling air of an icebox. In between the two sits the church missionary board engaging in the difficult task of trying to equalize the temperature. But that is merely a detail in passing.

The great fact to mark is that never has the missionary movement bulked so large. And never have such broad statesmanlike plans, such aggressiveness of spirit, coupled with deep devotion, marked the church in its great life-mission.

One morning at a popular summer resort on Long Island Sound thousands of bathers were enjoying the surf. The lifesaving crew were stationed for duty, on the lookout for any accident. A gentleman standing by one of the crew asked him how he could tell if help were needed. There were thousands of bathers, and a perfect babel of noises. The weather-beaten man, bronzed and toughened and trained to keenness in his work by years of service, said, "I can always hear a cry of distress, no matter how great the noise and confusion. There never yet has been a cry of need I haven't heard."

For a long time the confusion of noises bothered the ears of the church. But now the cry of distress from over the wide seas is being heard again distinctly, and is being responded to splendidly. The very earnestness of response and effort is a forerunner of sure victory.

A Great World Chorus

I recall vividly a scene in Albert Hall in London nearly fifteen years ago. A remarkable gathering from all parts of the world had come together. About two thousand men had arrived from the ends of the earth. It was a world gathering. There were sturdy Englishmen, cosmopolitan Americans, canny Scots, quick-witted Irishmen, sweet-voiced, fervid-spirited Welshmen, and courtly, suave Frenchmen.

Fair-haired, blue-eyed Scandinavians mingled with olive-skinned, black-eyed sons of Italy. The steady-going Hollander and the intense German mingled their deep voices with the songs of praise and the discussions. A few turbaned heads, inscrutably quiet almond eyes, and energetic step and speech brought to mind the Orient, India and China and Japan. Men won out of the savagery of Africa sat with Islanders from the Pacific.

They came from many communions and represented many creeds, and spoke as many tongues as did the Jerusalem crowds on the day of Pentecost. But they were drawn together not by their attractive diversity, but because of their oneness. The drawing power of Jesus was the magnet that drew them. It was the music of His name that made all their tongues and languages blend and chord in sweet harmony.

This night I speak of they had gathered in the great oval-shaped Albert Hall opposite Hyde Park. With the Londoners, probably ten thousand persons were present. And I think I shall never forget the vast volume of sound as, led by a chorus of Scandinavian students, they all united in singing, "All Hail the Power of Jesus' Name." They did not sing to the American tune of "Coronation," but to the old English "Miles Lane." That tune, you remember, in the last line, repeats four times the words, "crown Him," gradually increasing in volume and the fourth time touched with a bit of quieting awe.

I can close my eyes now, and see the great world gathering and hear again the sweet rhythmic thunder of their singing—

And crown Him,
Crown Him,
CROWN HIM,
Crown Him, Lord of all.

No one can tell to another the thrill of such a sight and sound. It was all unconsciously a bit of prophecy acted out, faint but distinct, of the great day of victory that is coming.

The Oratorio of Victory

Have you ever noticed the Oratorio of Revelation? Lovers of music should study the Book of Revelation of Saint John for its mighty choruses. It is striking just now to notice the double keynote of that closing climactic book of the Bible. It is this: Satan chained and Christ crowned. But note for a moment the oratorio sounding its music through the whole book.

It opens with a *solo* in the first chapter (Rev. 1: 5,6). John begins writing with steady pen until he seems to get a glimpse of Jesus. Then his pen drops the story, and he begins singing—

> Unto Him that loveth us,
> And loosed us from our sin by His own
> blood;
> And hath made us a kingdom of
> Priests unto His God and Father;
> To Him the glory and the dominion
> For ever and ever.

In chapter 4 comes a *Quartet* (v. 8). The four living creatures round about the throne take up the refrain of John's solo. And, as they sing, their song is caught up by a *Sextuple Quartet,* twenty-four white-robed, crowned men before the throne (Rev. 4:9–11; 5:8–10).

In chapter 5 the *Angel Chorus* swings in (vv. 11, 12). They are grouped round about the Quartet and the twenty-four elders. John begins to count them. Then his figures give out. His knowledge of mathematics is too limited. There were ten thousand times ten thousand, and unnumbered thousands of thousands. As far as his eye could see, to left and right, before and behind, was one vast sea of angel faces.

And John listened enraptured and awed, as their wondrous volume of rhythm rang and thundered out. Sweet sopranos and mellow contraltos, ringing tenors and deep basses; first one, then the other, back and forth responding to each other, then all together; marvelous music it must have been.

Then the refrain of their song is caught up by the *Creation Chorus* (Rev. 5:13). Every living creature in heaven and on the earth and under the earth, as though unable to resist the contagious sweep, catches up the music and adds his own to it. We do not commonly associate music with the animal creation, nor with nature. It has been said that all the sounds of nature are keyed in the minor, as though some suffering has affected them. We talk of the sighing of the wind, the moaning of the sea waves, and the mourning of the doves. (The singing birds must be excepted. They seem to have caught and kept some of the major strains.) But evidently something has occurred to strike a new keynote. For now they take up the refrain of the joyous song of the others, and increase the mighty song by their own.

In chapter 7 the music has ceased or softened down, and is taken up afresh by the *Martyr Chorus* (vv. 9–12). Again John's figures give out. He declares that nobody could count the multitudes that make up this chorus. It is a polyglot but all blend into full rhythm. It is a scarred chorus too. These have been through great tribulation. Their scars tell the mute story of the fierceness of the fight, and the steadiness of their faith.

Through their singing runs a distinct strain of

the minor. Its strangely sweet cadence, learned in many an hour of pain, runs as an undertone through the song of triumph that now fills their hearts and mouths. And as they sing, the Angel Chorus and the Quartet drop to their knees, and swell the wondrous refrain.

In chapter 14 comes the music of the *Chorus of Pure Ones* (vv. 1-5). They are gathered close about the person of Jesus. They sing to the accompaniment of a great company of harpers. They sing with a peculiar clearness in their tones. Theirs is a new song. Purity always makes a music of its own unapproachable for sweetness and clearness.

The *Victors' Chorus* rings out its song in Revelation 15:2-4. These have been in the thickest of the fighting. The smoke of the battle has darkened their faces. They have struggled with the enemy at close range, hip and thigh, nip and tuck, close parry and hard thrust. And they have come off victors. The ring of triumph resounds in their voices, as to the sound of their own harps, harps of God, they add their tribute of song to all the others.

And at the last comes the great *Hallelujah Chorus* (Rev. 19:1-8). In response to the precentor's call, they all join their voices in one vast melody. The Quartet, the Sextuple Quartet, the Angels, the Creation, the Martyrs, the Pure Ones, the Victors—all sing their song together.

John tries to tell what it was like. His mind goes quickly back to earlier days in his home city, Jerusalem, when thousands of pilgrims crowded the temple areas and narrow streets, and spread out over the hills. The unceasing sound of their voices in speech and in their pilgrim songs of praise comes back to him. He says the music of his vision was like that.

But that is not satisfactory. It is so much more. He thinks of how the ocean waves keep pounding with cannon roar on the rocky beach of his Patmos prison isle. He says the music was like that. But still more is needed to give an idea of the vast volume of sound. And he remembers how sometimes the thunders crashed and boomed and roared above him as he lay in his solitude on that lonely bit of sea-girt land. The music was like that. It was like all of these together.

And what is it they were singing? Well, there was variety in the wording of their song, as well as in their voices. But through all ran a refrain that brings back to my mind the great London chorus. It is this—

> And crown Him!
> *Crown Him!!*
> CROWN HIM!!!
> Yes, *crown Him*
> Lord of all.

This is the rehearsal of the great Oratorio of Victory that we are all to join in singing.

7

The Church

Forces That Win

God's world is full of winning forces. The great ball of fire around which our earth revolves is the greatest winning force in the life of the earth. It is constantly winning the earth to itself with a power unseen but tremendous, beyond anybody's power to calculate. The swing of the earth away from the sun is being continually overcome. By an immense drawing power the sun steadily holds the earth where it can pour down its wealth of warmth and light and life into it.

The sun woos the moisture up from river and lake and sea, until its gravity partner in the center of the earth woos the moisture back again in refreshing rain and sheltering snow. The sun wins out of the earth's warm heart bounteous harvests of grains and fruits, the wealth of forests which affects the earth's life so radically, the flowers with their beauty and fragrance, and the soft carpeting of green to ease the journey for our feet. All the life and beauty of the earth are due to the winning power of the sun.

God Himself is the greatest winning force in all our world. Everywhere men feel the upward drawing toward Him. They may protest against church organizations and creeds, against teachings and long-settled practices and habits of thought, as they do so much, but there is always everywhere a longing in the human heart for God. It is the answer to the longing of His heart for us.

And man is a great winning force. Everywhere men are attracted to each other. There is a winning power within each of us that draws certain others irresistibly to us. And there are winning forces in life that each one of us is powerfully affected by. The old home of earlier days has a marvelous power of attraction for most men. The old fireside, the familiar rooms, the subtle aroma that seems inseparable from the very bricks and boards—who has not felt the tremendous drawing power of these?

What a strange power of attraction a man's mother-tongue has for him. How the heart will give a quick leap, in a foreign land, when, amid a confusing jargon of strange sounds, all unexpectantly someone speaks dear old familiar words. The person speaking may not be specially congenial or attractive to us, but that sound his tongue gives draws us to him.

God's Law of Leadership

Now I want to talk with you about the forces at hand for winning our old world back to our Father's heart and home. God means us to use all the attractive powers we have in this great world-wooing and world-winning task. The world is to be *won* back, not driven. Men drive men when they can. But God woos and wins. Man's coming back must be by his own glad, sweet consent. God will not have it any other way.

There are certain strangely winsome forces at our command for winning man. They are mighty in their drawing power. But there are counter-currents that divert and hinder their influence. We need to be familiar with these winning forces, and with the countercurrents too.

There are seven great forces at our command for this blessed service of soul-winning and world-winning. They are not peculiar to foreign mission service, for the foreign service itself is not essentially different from other service, except in the greatness of its need. They are the forces for use in all our winning work.

Two of these are distinctly human forces. The first is an organization, *the church*. And then that of which the church is made up, *men and women;* I mean the power of personality, developed and consecrated personality.

There are two divine forces that work through the human—*Jesus* and the *Holy Spirit*. I have put these after the human forces, because they work through the human. The leadership is in human hands. *The initiative of all action is with us.* Of course, if you go a bit deeper in, the initiative is with God, who moves upon our hearts to make us act. But on the distinctly human level the beginning of service rests in human hands, and these two mighty, almighty, divine forces work through us.

The divine law of leadership and of cooperation in leadership has not always been clearly understood. And there has often been bad delay because of the lack of understanding. Our Lord Jesus in the days of His humanity surrendered Himself to the leadership of the Holy Spirit in His great mission to men. The Spirit worked through Jesus. After Jesus' ascension the order was reversed. The Spirit yielded Himself to the control of the glorified Son of God. Jesus worked through the Spirit. It was Jesus who sent down the Holy Spirit on the day of Pentecost for the special mission begun that day.

And now, with the greatest awe coming into our hearts at the thought, be it said that these two work through our human leadership. The leadership in service among men is human leadership. The wondrous Spirit of God works through our leadership to reveal Jesus to men in all His winsomeness and power.

There can be no power at all in our human action and leadership except as the Spirit leads and controls us, and is allowed to. And, on the other side, we must not forget, though it has sometimes been forgotten, that God's working waits upon human action and leadership. Memory quickly brings up the fact, so often repeated in the history of the church, that when men have failed to respond to God's call His work has fallen behind. Whenever a new chapter of earnest service has been begun, it has always been through a new leadership. Some man has listened to God, and let Him have the free use of himself in reaching out to other men.

God needs men. He needs you and me. We are the wire for the transmission of His current of power. The wire is useless without the current. And the current must have the wire along which to travel to its place of service. The divine power works through human action and human leadership. The power is all divine. And the means through which it works is all human. Jesus and the Holy Spirit work through the church, and through each one of us who is willing.

Rounding out the seven forces at our command are *prayer, money,* and *sacrifice.*

God's Messenger

In this chapter we want to talk about the first of the two human forces—the church. We ought to remind ourselves of just what that word *church* means in this connection. It has many meanings. There are at least two that we should note here in thinking of it as a great winning force. In its broadest meaning the word is commonly used for the whole group of church organizations taken together, the Roman Catholic and the Greek Orthodox, the Protestant, and the few primitive societies that still retain their old original organization. In the deeper, less used meaning it stands for the body of those men and women everywhere who are trusting Jesus Christ, and are allied with Him in the purpose of their hearts.

Jesus planned that His church should be a great man-winning and world-winning organization. *The* mission of the church is to take Jesus to all men. It is God's messenger of His truth to all. In that respect it is the direct lineal descendant and heir of the Hebrew nation.

That nation was chosen to be a messenger or missionary nation. That was the one purpose of its special creation as a nation. It was not to be as the other nations, in the characteristics that commonly mark strong nations. It was to be a *teacher*-nation, receiving its message of truth directly from God, embodying that message in its own life, personally and nationally, and giving it out clearly and fully and winsomely to all the nations of the earth. And, in spite of its failures and breaks, that mission was accomplished to a remarkable extent.

The church is Israel's heir. It was born in the Jewish nation. It became the heir to its worldwide messenger mission. The Great Commission given by Jesus as He was about to ascend is the church's commission for its great lifework. It was spoken to the group of Jewish men who were to be the nucleus of that body called the church, which came into being on the day of Pentecost. That ringing "Go ye into all the world and preach my gospel to the whole creation" is the Master's command to the church which He brought into being. That is the church's marching order by which its life is to be controlled and its faithfulness judged.

The scene of the church's birth gives a vivid picture of its world mission. It was born in a world gathering. It was a world church in its makeup at its birth. Men from all parts of the world became united in one body by the Spirit's touch on the birthday of the church. Its birth-gift, the power of speaking many tongues, reveals at once the wide sweep of its service.

It was the Master's plan that His church should speak all the languages of the earth then and now and always, as well as the language of heaven, the language of love. Thus every man would learn of Jesus in his native speech. The language of the cradle and of lovemaking and of the fireside, the language that most quickly kindles the fires in a man's heart, that is the language to be used in carrying Jesus to every man. That is Jesus' plan.

Of course, this is not the only mission of the church. That is to say, there are other purposes necessarily included in it. Taking the gospel of Jesus to all men means more than merely taking it and telling it. The teaching and training and developing of those won to Jesus are an inseparable part of the church's mission. The great service of worship has always been recognized as a vital part of the church's life. Sometimes indeed these have been thought of, and still are thought of, as its only mission. But they grow distinctly out of the chief mission and are contributory and secondary to it. Indeed, they come into being only through the faithful doing of the chief task. Men were won. Then they met for worship and for training.

Everybody—Everywhere!

The church of those first years thoroughly understood what its great mission was to be. The first chapters of the Book of Acts vividly describe the ideal church as planned by the Master, and as understood by those who felt His own personal touch upon themselves. *Everybody went.* They went to everybody. They went everywhere. There is clear evidence that they actually went everywhere that men could go. They held their lives, and even their property, subject to the one great gripping purpose.

The greatest leader of the first century of the church, Paul, who contributed most of its literature and exerted the greatest influence upon its life, was above all else a missionary leader. He went practically everywhere. He did not go hastily, but by carefully thought out plans. He won men to Christ, organized them into church assemblies, taught them, and sent them out to win others.

Paul worked in and out of the world's great city centers of his time. Ephesus, the Asiatic center; Corinth, the center of Greek influence; and Rome, the center of the world's governing power, were the scenes of his longest and most thorough campaigns. His choice of these centers was masterly strategy. For these centers sent their influence out to the ends of the earth. Paul's body might be in Ephesus or Corinth or Rome, but his thought and heart were on the world these cities reached by constant streams of influence.

And to these churches which he had won out of the raw stuff of heathenism he taught the same worldwide message. They became filled with this same worldwide spirit. The Thessalonian and Corinthian churches made their winning power felt throughout Greece and wherever Greek culture had gone, that is to say, everywhere (I Thess. 1-8; II Cor. 1:1). The church in Rome sent the message of Jesus out from its golden center along all Roman roads, out to the farthest reaches of the Roman Empire (Rom. 1:8).

It is striking, though not surprising, that the days of the church's missionary activity have been the days of its greatest purity and vigor. When the vision of the Master's face on Olivet and the ringing sound of His "Go ye" have been lost, the church has written pages that would gladly be blotted out.

The church *has* been a winning force beyond any power of calculation or words of description.

All that has been done has been done through its activity and leadership. It is today a tremendous winning force, reaching its warm hands out to the very ends of the earth, and drawing men to Jesus. With our earnest prayer it will exert a yet mightier influence in taking Jesus to all men and in winning men everywhere to Jesus.

Change the World

David Livingstone, one of the church's great world-winning pioneers, was once lost in the depths of equatorial Africa. That is to say, he had advanced so far ahead of everybody else that the rest of us lost track of him, and so we called him lost. Perhaps we got the use of the word twisted, and we were the lost ones because we had not kept up. He had gone where the church was told to go, but the rest of us had lingered behind, and so the main column became detached from its leader. Everybody was talking about the lost leader.

James Gordon Bennett, the owner of the *New York Herald,* sent a telegram to one of its correspondents, Henry M. Stanley. Bennett was in Paris, and Stanley at Gibraltar. The telegram summoned Stanley to come to Paris at once. Stanley went, reached Paris at midnight, knocked at the great newspaperman's door, and asked what was wanted. "Find Livingstone" was the short, blunt reply. "How much money do you place at my disposal?" asked Stanley. "Fifty thousand dollars, or a larger sum. Never mind about the money; find Livingstone."

Stanley went. It took two years' time to get ready. It required a specially planned campaign and thorough preparation. The planning was done, and the world was thrilled when the bold missionary leader was found.

Our Master has sent a message to His church. It is written down in a Book, and is being repeated constantly. He says, "Find my world and change it! Bring it back to me; never mind about the expense of money and lives. *Find my world, and win it back.*" And the church has the power to do so.

8

Prayer

The Greatest Thing

The greatest of all things we can *do* is *pray*.

Jesus lived a life of prayer. All that He did and said grew out of His prayer. There is no way of knowing exactly to what extent this held true. But the more I study His life the stronger grows the impression that His teaching, preaching, and healing activities, which form the greater part of the Gospel pages, were actually less than His praying. He seems to have put prayer first. All the rest was an outgrowth of it. He was on a world-changing errand. And this was what He thought of prayer. *The emphasis of Jesus' personal habit was laid upon prayer.*

The Holy Spirit is a Spirit of prayer. He is the Master Intercessor. He breathes into us the spirit of prayer, and makes it glow into a passion. He teaches us how to pray. This is a lifelong teaching. You who are teachers know that patience and skill are more essential to a good teacher than is the knowledge taught. With greatest skill and loving, tactful patience the Spirit teaches us to pray.

And then He does more: He uses each of us as His prayer closet, praying in us with yearnings beyond utterance the prayer to which we have not yet reached up, but which needs to be prayed down on the earth. All the power needed in the great world-changing work is in the Holy Spirit and comes from Him. *And the chief thing He emphasizes is prayer.*

The greatest thing each one of us can do is to pray. If we can go personally to some distant land, still we have gone to only one place. *But our field is the world.* It is impossible for us to reach our whole field personally. But it can be reached, and reached effectually, by prayer. The place where you and I are sent, whether at home or abroad, is simply our *base of action.* It is our field for *personal* touch. And that means very much. But it is only a small part of our field of activity. It is most significant as our *base of action,* from which we send out our secret messengers of prayer to all parts of the field.

And then, in the particular town or city or country district to which we have been sent, or in which we are being kept, the prayer properly comes before the personal activity. And it runs side by side with the activity, and follows along after. We give the personal touch which must be given, and which may be so marvelous in power, but there is something even there greater than the personal touch; and that is the power of prayer.

It is through prayer that the personal presence means most. That personal presence may become a hindrance. It may be a drag upon the work. It often is just that for lack of prayer. For the real sweetness and efficiency of personal service out among men are in secret prayer.

And if we give *money*, there is even greater need for prayer to go with it. Money seems almost almighty. As a winning force, of course, it must be reckoned far less than personal service. For it is less. It gets its almost omnipotence from human hands. If the personal touch depends for its subtle power on prayer, how much more does money! Money given to missions, unaccompanied by prayer, can no doubt be made to do great good. But it is a very pauper alongside a small amount of money that is charged with the spirit-current of prayer.

At the Other End

One day I ran across a party of about twenty men from Pittsburgh on their way to a Christian convention in Cincinnati. There were a few ministers in the party, but it was made up chiefly of businessmen, typical, keen, alert American businessmen. We got together and talked about things of common interest.

And this question was asked: *Does prayer do*

things? Then the question was spread out some. I go into my room at night to retire. I read a passage from God's Book, and kneel to pray. I pray for a man in Pittsburgh or in Hangchow, China. Does anything take place in Pittsburgh or in Hangchow that would not have taken place if I had not prayed? Of course, the praying does *me* good. The very bending of knee and head before God, the good wishes in my heart going out to someone else—these influence me. I rise better for both.

But is that all? Does anything happen *at the other end?* Does my prayer do anything in Hangchow? If I write a business letter to Hangchow, enclosing a foreign draft, the letter does something. A vast amount of business is carried on in that way. Does the prayer do something as real as do the letter and the draft?

There was a good deal of talk back and forth, and questions asked. It was interesting to find these men were ready to admit that they really believed that something would occur at the other end. They belonged to a church noted for its sound teaching on these important spiritual matters. The matter-of-fact power of prayer to do business "at the other end" seemed to appeal to these businessmen. Apparently they had not been looking at prayer that way. But they readily admitted that it must be so. Then the next question asked itself: How much of this foreign business are we doing? And so the little crowd talked along while the train pounded the rails at the rate of forty-odd miles an hour.

Prayer does do things. Something happens at the other end that would not happen if the prayer were not made. The banker, carrying out his business, can touch London and Paris and Shanghai and Calcutta and Tokyo, without moving from the desk where he is dictating letters, with his correspondence spread out before him. The praying man can as readily touch these cities as he kneels in his room, with a world map and God's Book spread out before him.

Doing Business

I use that word *business* in this connection thoughtfully and reverently. I know there is a sacredness, a hallowedness about prayer that never or rarely enters into business matters. We keep the two things apart in our thoughts, reckoning the one a common thing, and the other a holy thing. And I would increase, if I could, that sense of reverence in prayer. But there is a great advantage in using the familiar language of business in thinking of the results of our praying.

Prayer is doing business for God. To think in that way gives a practicality, a sense of something you can touch and feel. Shall we not make plans at once to increase our foreign correspondence?

You can have a simple schedule or memorandum to guide your praying. I do not mean a slavish hard-and-fast system, or set of rules, set down to be followed, with a feeling that you have been untrue if you forget. Nothing of that sort at all. But merely a simple something to glance at each day, and so serve as a reminder to guide your thoughts.

A little memorandum can be made which runs through the days of the week. It can be so planned as to run around the world during the week. The little schedule which I use is divided into the days of the week, Sunday to Saturday. For each day there is a page containing notes and catchwords about personal affairs, and home, and friends, and church, and appointments, and such items. Then each day of the week has a page on which are marked homeland items and foreign items.

A little prayer book of that sort grows under constant use. Your reading of missionary news leads to the making of fresh notes. Names of persons are added, and dates of coming conferences, and so on, and verses of Scripture that stand out in the daily reading. So the book becomes to you a very precious little batch of leaves, lying inside the precious Book of God.

The prayer book should be accompanied by a map of the world.[1] For a good while I used a map which was inserted in one of Dr. A. T. Pierson's mission books. That map has long since been replaced by others, which are larger and give

[1]World Literature Crusade, P.O. Box 1313, Studio City, California 91604, makes available a special World Prayer Map for Christians interested in focusing prayer on the nations of the world.

more information. It is an immense help to glance at the map daily, and look at the part marked for the day. The lands get fixed in mind in that way without special effort. Gradually they stand out more and more clearly, and come to be very real to you.

The map may become dear to you, for it suggests the field that you are influencing. It is your prayer sailing-chart. It becomes fragrant with memories. Experiences you have had alone with God over His Word, and over this map of His world, come back to refresh and sweeten.

Prayer: A Habit

There is a little sentence of Paul's that used to puzzle and bother me, "Pray without ceasing." But it has become a great help to me. It puzzled me because I did not see any practical way of doing it. Paul's counsel does not seem to mean the repetition of prayers, with little mechanical helps, such as some use. It surely does not mean staying on your knees twenty-four hours each day. But, as I tried to pray my way into its meaning, it came to mean four distinct things to me. Prayer is a habit, an attitude, a life, a person. And I would not be surprised to find more yet coming out of Paul's admonition.

First of all, Paul means that prayer should be *a habit.* There should be a fixed time (or times) every day for going off alone to pray. Into that time God's Word is taken. Quiet time is spent in reading it. For this is listening to God. And that comes first in praying: listening first, then speaking. The reading may be rapid and broad, or slower and more meditative. Whichever it may be, there should be a cultivation of *the habit of meditation.*

By the habit of meditation I do not mean a sleepy trying to imitate what we suppose some holy men do. But a keen thinking into the meaning of the words, and into their practical use in one's own life. As for the praying itself, we should be still before God, and make definite intercession for particular things, and persons, and places. That habit can be fixed until it becomes second nature. It can be cultivated until it becomes the sweet spot of the day to you.

Prayer: An Attitude

Then while the daily habit continues, prayer may become an attitude, *a bent of mind.* Whatever comes up suggests prayer to you. The bent of your mind is to pray as things come up in the daily round. You cannot stop your work, but you *think* prayers. Your heart prays while your hands are busy.

I shall never forget the school in which I learned to pray this way. A case of protracted illness in my home required my personal attention constantly for a time. It seemed as if no assistance I could get meant quite as much as what I could do personally. The life in peril was so precious that all else dropped out of sight. My habits of life were completely broken up. I was up night and day. Even the early morning hour of reading and prayer was broken into.

But as I went about my round of service, I found myself praying constantly. I was much wearied, and things sometimes seemed desperate. I realized how everything depended on God's touch. And without any planning a habit of continual praying formed itself. I could be engaged in conversation, thinking intently about something needing great care, and yet there was an undercurrent of prayer constantly. I shall never cease to be grateful for that trying experience, because in it this new habit of a praying bent of mind formed itself.

Do you know how as you go about your ordinary round there is a constant undercurrent of thought? You may be talking, or reading, or writing, or doing something more mechanical, and yet this train of thought is running along apparently of its own accord, regardless of you. It is broken at times, or you lose consciousness of it, as your work requires closer attention. When you swing into the habitual things that you have done over and over again until they almost do themselves, it reasserts itself.

I remember years ago, in a banking house where I served for a time, I had long additions to make. Sometimes the rows of figures to be added up were a foot in length. And I got so used to adding that often I was surprised to find that my thoughts had been far away, completely taken up with something else, while I had been adding the figures. And fearing that I had been slighting my work, I would go back carefully all over the figures, only to find the totals correct. The adding habit had become fixed, and left the undercurrent of my thought free.

That current is apt to reveal the heart's purpose or set of mind. Whatever you are most set upon, whatever your favorite fads or hobbies or inclinations or moods are, they are apt to appear in that involuntary train of thinking. Now this can be cultivated. It can be cultivated chiefly by developing the controlling purpose of your life, and then by trying to give direction to the undercurrent, and holding it to that direction. If Jesus has gripped your heart, the purpose of your life will be for Him. And if you have come to realize the tremendous power of prayer, this undercurrent of thought can be made a prayer-current.

I am not advocating an artificial holding of one's self to such a current by dint of force, and then mentally whipping yourself if you have forgotten. The power of all action lies in its being perfectly free and natural. You can cultivate a passion for Jesus, a life purpose, and a prayer habit; and all of this will be a training of that undercurrent of thought toward prayer.

The shipping clerk, as he heads his barrels and boxes, can be sending out and up his current of prayer. At intervals he is thinking closely about something connected with his work. Then his thoughts free themselves. As he hammers in the nails, his thought says, "This is China day."

Each ringing blow of the hammer rings out, "This is China day. Let Thy blessing, Master, rest today upon believers in Hangchow, and upon Mr. Blank out there; may there be victory in Jesus' name today; may gospel booklets and Bibles be distributed. Grant Thy power and help to the national workers."

The picture of the shipping clerk's little prayer memorandum comes up before his mind's eye. The map of China stands out more or less distinctly, depending on how long he may have been looking at it in his prayer hour. His mind runs of itself from one point to another. And so, all the while, his undercurrent of prayer goes on. It is broken into by newer or more exacting duties; then it is free again, swinging more or less to what his heart is set upon. This becomes a perfectly free, natural habit with him. And here we see part of the meaning of Paul's admonition to "pray without ceasing."

Prayer: A Life

Then prayer is a *life*. The life is what you are in yourself. It is not the mere span of years you live through. Your thoughts and loves, your heart's ambitions and intense purposes, the things you will to do, and to be—that is your life. It exerts an enormous influence upon the circle in which you live, and upon the world. Ideas don't change the world; people do.

If underneath all else that driving purpose,

that warm, intense love-power, that yearning desire, is Godward, and manward, and world-ward, it becomes a prayer, a continual prayer. You are not thinking of it that way. But that is your life, and that life is a prayer. Its influence against the evil one and for God is enormous. It changes the world.

It is a prayer unceasing, as long and as strong as your life itself. Satan fears it. It hinders him and thwarts him every day. The fragrant incense from the censer of your life rises up before the throne of God continually, and affects the events on the earth (Rev. 8:3–5).

Prayer: A Person

And then prayer is a *person*. That is to say, you yourself may be a prayer, a walking prayer offered up in Jesus' name. Your presence will affect the evil one, and change events, and help God in His plans. You may be so allied with Jesus in the simple, intense purpose of your heart that you yourself, where you are, by your mere presence, will be recognized by evil spirits, and by the Master Himself as a mighty power for God.

Your presence disturbs the evil one's plan. It has an influence upon those you meet. It is helping God alter the course of nations. The whole effect of your presence is precisely the same as a prayer. You are a prayer yourself, though unconsciously. The whole trend of your life says,

"Thy Kingdom come; Thy will be done on earth as in heaven."

Years ago President Theodore Roosevelt's daughter was a member of the Taft party that visited parts of the Orient. She did not go as the president's daughter, of course. There could be no official significance attached to her presence. We Americans can understand better than some others that she went simply as a young woman eager to see Japan and China, not as the president's daughter.

But everywhere she went in the Orient she was treated not merely as a member of a touring group, but as the daughter of the President of the United States. Presents were given to her, receptions tendered, and deference shown, because of her personal relation to her father. To the Orientals her presence stood for the head of our government. Their treatment of her reflected the fact that she was his daughter.

Even so it is with us Christians. The evil one does not think of you and me simply as individuals. He thinks of us in relation to Jesus, who is his Conqueror. He fears us as he fears Jesus. That is, he can be made to fear us, by our being true to our Lord.

The final purpose of prayer is to defeat Satan and to bring about God's will. And we do just that in our persons, by our presence; or we may. Prayer is a person. You are a prayer. The man himself becomes a tremendous prayer, offsetting evil influences, changing men and events, and helping God in His plans.

These last two, the life and the person, may be called unconscious prayer. The influence is constantly going out, though we are not aware of it. But it is great encouragement to recall that this prayer power is going out of us constantly. And these two are not limited to the place where we are. They act as a momentum to every wish we breathe, and every spoken prayer we utter, sending these with renewed force out to the place we have in mind. Spiritual influence does not know anything about the limitations of distance.

Unseen Changes

All this praying makes a difference at the other end, the place toward which it is directed. Things in Shanghai are made different. The copy of a gospel booklet that some national in West Bengal, India, is reading becomes a living missionary because of this praying. Your prayer is a spirit-force traveling instantly through the distance between you and the place for which you are praying. And things occur that otherwise would not.

Opposition lessens. Difficulties give way. The road some man is traveling clears and brightens. The truth on the printed page stands out in bigger letters. The health of a Christian worker renews. The sickness or weakness gives way to a new health and strength. The judgment steers a straight course. The purpose holds its anchor steady. The man rides the rough seas of spiritual difficulty safely.

Things are happening. And they are happening because a handful of scarcely noticed intercessors, some older, some younger, are giving themselves to the unselfish ministry of reclaiming the world for Christ's eternal kingdom. As Frances Havergal wrote:

> There are noble Christian workers,
> The men of faith and power,
> The overcoming wrestlers
> Of many a midnight hour;
> Prevailing princes with their God,
> Who will not be denied,
> Who bring down showers of blessing
> To swell the rising tide.
> The Prince of Darkness quaileth
> At their triumphant way,
> *Their fervent prayer availeth*
> *To sap his subtle sway.*

9

Money

Limitations

Money seems almost almighty in its power to do things and make changes. It can make a desert blossom as a rose. It can even defy death. Medical skill holds the life here that otherwise would have been snuffed out. Great buildings go up. Colleges begin their life with apparatus and books, skilled instructors, and eager students. Mammoth enterprises spring into being. Hospitals and churches rise up with skilled attendants and talented preachers.

We have come, in our day, and perhaps peculiarly in our country, to think that there is no limit to the power of money. Our ideas of its value are really greatly exaggerated. That first sentence I used would be revised by many to read, "Money is almighty." The cautious words *seems* and *almost* would be promptly cut out.

Yet money has great limitations. It will help greatly to remember what they are. And many of us need the brain-clearing of that help. Of itself money is utterly useless, so much deadweight stuff lying useless and helpless. It must have human hands to make it valuable. It gets its value from our conception of its value and from our use of it. It must have a human partner to be of any service at all.

In bad hands it becomes devilish in its badness. And I need not put an "almost" in that sentence. It may be as a very demon, or as the arch-devil himself, just as at times it may seem to be divine in its creative and changing power.

Then it is valuable only in this world, on the earth. At the line of death its value wholly ceases. Over that line it takes its place as a pauper. It is represented as being used for cobblestones in the streets of the New Jerusalem. Yet it would need to go through some hardening process to make it of any account at all as paving material.

We ought to remind ourselves of something else, too, that the crowd constantly forgets, and that we are tempted to forget when touched by the contagion of the crowd. And that is, that money is always less in its power than is a strong, sweet, pure life. Maybe you think that comparison cannot properly be made. You say that things so unlike cannot be compared. But, whether consciously and intentionally or otherwise, that comparison is being made constantly in practical life, and most times to the advantage of money. Commonly the crowd reckons money more than character.

We do well to remind ourselves that its influence for good is always distinctly less than that of a life. To live a life pure and strong and wholesome in its ideals out among men is more than to be able to give money in any amount. To keep one's life up to such ideals in the heartless drive and competition of modern life means more than to extract large quantities of gold out of the mine of barter and trade, and to give some of it away.

The Best Partnership

Give money good partners, and there is no end to what it can do. Let prayer and sacrifice and money form a life-partnership, and that first sentence can be revised, and greatly strengthened by the revision. Money *is* almost almighty. It gets all the good qualities of its partners as long as it stays in the partnership, on good working terms.

It is not the head of the firm, however. Prayer belongs in that place. It must direct. It is the prayer's touch with God that hallows the gold and gives to it some of God's omnipotence. Money is the working partner, best when hard at work, and famous for the amount of work it can do in obeying orders from the head of the house.

It gives a strange sense of awe to realize that the small amount of money you hold in your hand can be used to *change a life,* aye, more, to change many lives. That money is yours to control. It came to you in exchange for your labor or your skill. It is yours, for the sweat of your brow or your brain is upon it. And now it can be sent out, and the result will be a life utterly changed, purified, and redeemed.

Through your partnership the money produces something greater than itself. And that changed life becomes the center of a new power, changing other lives out to the far rim of an ever-widening circle. It may have cost you much. Some of your very life has gone out in the work that brought into your hands that bit of gold. It is red with your blood. And now, if you choose, it can be sent out and made to bring new life to someone else. Life has gone from you in getting it, and life will come to another in your giving it out, under the blessed Master's transmitting touch.

The Master's Teaching

Christ's teaching about money is startling. I mean that it stands in such utter contrast to the commonly accepted standards out in the world, and even inside in the church, that the contrast startles one sharply.

There are four passages in which Christ teaches about money. There is the "lay not up for yourselves treasures upon earth" passage in the Sermon on the Mount (Matt. 6:19-21), and the still stronger phrase in the Luke parallel, "Sell that ye have and give" (12: 33, 34). There are the incident of the earnest young man who was rich

(Matt. 19:16–30; Mark 10:17–31; Luke 18:18–30); the parable of the wealthy farmer in Luke's twelfth chapter (vv. 13–21); and the whole sixteenth chapter of Luke, with that great ninth verse, whose full meaning has been so little grasped. The truth taught in each of these passages is practically the same thing.

The Master is evidently talking about what a man has over and above his personal and family needs. It is a law of life, from Eden on, that a man should work to supply his daily needs and the needs of those dependent upon him. Just how much that word *needs* means, each man settles for himself. It even means different things at different times to the same man.

It is surprising how little the word *needs* can be made to mean when the pinch comes, and yet a man still have all actual necessities supplied. The man who would have his life count most for the Master and the Master's plan thinks over that word prayerfully and sensibly with full regard to personal strength, and loved ones, and the future. Whatever the word may be made to mean, Christ's teaching is plainly about what is left over after the needs are met.

Now, about that leftover amount the Master gives three easily understood rules, or bits of advice, or commands. First: *Do not treasure it up for the sake of having it.* If you do, it is in danger, and you are in danger. It may be stolen. Every vault, and safe, and safety-deposit company, and lock and key back up that statement. Or it may be lost to rust or moths, two things that threaten all inactivity. The stuff that is not in use wears away. The wear of use cannot compare with the wear of disuse or neglect.

Then *you* are in danger of your heart's being affected. *It will be wherever your treasure is.* It may get locked up, and so dry up for lack of air or be poisoned by bad air. The blood must have fresh air. The heart must have touch with men to keep its vigor. It may get all dried up by contact solely with *things,* instead of keeping vigorous by touch with needy men. That is the twofold danger. The first thing Jesus says, then, is: Do not store your money up, down here, in the ordinary way.

The second thing is this: *Store your surplus up.* Be careful of it. Keep strict tally. Let the books be well kept and balanced. Let no thoughtlessness nor carelessness nor thriftlessness get in. Store it up. *But be careful where you store it.* Keep it carefully guarded against the action of thieves and moths, and against the inaction of decaying, destroying rust. That is the second thing. Store it up carefully.

The third thing is this: *Store up the surplus by means of exchange.* Keep it safe by giving it away. The whole value of money is in exchange. It must be kept moving. But—and the whole heart of the teaching is here—be very wary about your exchanges. Invest your money in *men,* wherever the need may be. All that you invest wisely in men is stored up against any violence or craftiness of thieves and any corroding of rust. A thief can rob a bank wherein we hoard our investment, but he cannot rob the gospel seed from the heart of a man. To give to lost men is to store up our investments in heaven.

All money not out in active use directly among men, for men, in Jesus' name, is in danger of being stolen, or of decaying, or of injuring you, or of being left behind, utterly worthless to you when you die. Be your own executor.

Some years ago one of the religious periodicals of New York City told of the death of a maiden lady named Elizabeth Pellit. Her home was in the hall of a tenement house, and at her death all her earthly possessions could be put into one trunk. No executor or administrator was needed. In view of her narrow circumstances, her friends thought she had denied herself all luxuries and even many comforts. But in the forty years of her Christian life she had been able to give over thirty thousand dollars to missionary work. She had supplied the money to send out and sustain one missionary in Salvador, and also for another who was to go out soon. She seemed to have grasped the meaning of the Master's teaching.

Good common sense comes in for free play here, both in adjusting one's personal and family schedule and in giving. Giving may be done foolishly, not wisely. There is no place where there is more room for good sense in avoiding both the extreme of unwise giving and the other extreme of handicapping one's gifts.

It is a question of personal judgment how far to

give money out directly and how far to invest some of it and use the income wholly in gifts. You may think that in some directions you can invest it better, and direct the income better than can some church organizations. That may be true. But the chief thing is that the money itself be dedicated wholly for use out among lost men.

Now you will please mark keenly that in all this I am not talking about what I think about money. I am simply putting into plain talk Christ's own teaching about it, in these four great passages.

Missing the Meaning

Christian men, generally, seem to have missed the meaning of Christ's words. I think this is due largely to the lack of teaching in the church that world evangelism is a *first* obligation.

Recently a fire destroyed the home of a man of large wealth who lives some distance east of San Francisco. It was a beautiful palace, full of art treasures. The value of house and furnishings and the art collection was reckoned at about two million dollars. He is a Christian man, prominently identified with active Christian work, and reckoned a liberal giver. He has visited foreign missions, and made special gifts to them.

But in contrast with the two million dollars tied up for himself in the house that burned his gifts to missions seem like a copper cent or a silver quarter given to a beggar. Two millions stored up in a home, while many millions of men have lived and died in ignorance of the light and peace that come with Jesus! Yet this man calls Jesus his Master, and, sincerely; I do not doubt his sincerity. Yet his Master said the one great thing was to tell all men of His love and death.

By no extension of the meaning of that word *need* could anyone be said to need a two million dollar home for himself and family. And there are other millions under the same man's control. It looks very much as if this good man has missed the meaning of Jesus' words. The criticism, however, must be first upon the church and its leaders, with whose general trend of teaching this man is in accord. According to the Master's teaching, most of the money tied up in his house, and stored up in similar ways for himself, is being lost. Far more serious, the opportunity of investment in men is being lost. That money will be all loss to him when he reaches the line of departure into the next sphere of life.

It is very difficult to use such an illustration from life. There is danger that the words will sound critical in a bad or unkind sense. I earnestly pray to be kept from that. You will know that I am talking to myself first of all, and that I am speaking of this only to help. The tragedy is that this man is not an exception. Rather, he represents the habit and standard of his generation.

I recall another Christian man as I speak, of

large wealth, by inheritance and by dint of business keenness. His face showed plainly his fine Christian character. He gave liberally in many directions, sometimes very large sums. But he lived in a home whose value ran close to a half million dollars. When he died, full of years and honors, he left many millions to a son who did not inherit his father's generous hand with his wealth. Of course, the son did not *need* the vast wealth in the first place.

And I wondered, silently, within my heart, how things looked to that man, as he slipped out of life up into the Master's presence, and looked down on the earth through the eyes of the One whose teaching we have been talking about. He could see China, India, and Africa then as plainly as the United States of America.

How did the lost opportunity of laying up his treasure in the lives of men look to him then, I wondered. He was a good man. I saw him smile once, and his face seemed to shine as an angel's. I think probably no faithful friend had ever talked to him of the plain meaning of Jesus' words, and of world evangelism being a *first* obligation. He had not been taught this from the pulpit. And he had not discovered the secret for himself.

Money Talks

Many are losing a great opportunity of silently preaching Jesus to their fellows by their habit of giving. Two farmers were discussing the evidences of the Christian religion. The one was a Christian; the other was inclined to be skeptical. Arguments were freely exchanged. At last the skeptic, who was a blunt, outspoken man, said frankly to his friend and neighbor: "I think we might as well drop this matter. For I don't believe a word you say. And, more than that, I am quite satisfied in my own mind that you do not really believe it yourself. For to my certain knowledge you have not given, over the last twenty years, as much for the spread of Christianity as your last Durham cow cost. Why, sir, if I believed what you say you believe, I'd make the church my rule for giving, my farm the exception."

That Christian man's life was contradicting every word he uttered to his neighbor. Money talks. His was talking very loudly to his skeptical neighbor. His neighbor was unusually frank in saying aloud what thousands are thinking. That Christian had lost a great opportunity of winning his friend.

Debts

In a simple little sentence Paul reveals how thoroughly he had grasped the heart of Christ's teaching. He said, "*I am debtor* both to Greeks and barbarians"—to all men (Rom. 1:14). Now that word *debtor* commonly involves two things:

that you have received something of value from someone, and that therefore you owe him for what he gave you.

But Paul had not received anything special from the men of whom he was speaking. His birth and training and whatever else he had were Jewish. And the Jews were a minority in the world. He was not under a debtor's obligation of having received something from the men he was speaking of.

In Paul's understanding, the word *debt* involves *three* things: first, something received from God (and that something is everything); second, something owing to God; and third, that something *payable to man*. Paul counted himself in debt to all men on Jesus' account. And so are we. How much do *you* owe to your Lord? That is how much you are to pay to men on your Lord's account.

We do not even own ourselves, much less the goods we claim to possess. We were purchased when we were bankrupt. A great price was paid for us, even the lifeblood of Jesus. And our owner bids us pay our debt by giving to help others. We are badly and blessedly in debt: badly, for we can never square the account; blessedly, because we can be constantly paying on the account, out to others in Jesus' great name.

Is not that the meaning of Paul's "Owe no man anything, save to love one another" (Rom. 13:8)? We owe a debt of love to all men on Jesus' account. We can be paying on it continually, and yet never get a receipt in full that discharges the debt. But then we get other things in full—peace, and joy, and a life overflowing in fulness.

With an honorable businessman *a debt is a first obligation*. His personal expenditures and standard of living are shaped by his debt. The extras that he would otherwise feel quite free in allowing himself and his family are not allowed until the debt is cleared. The debt controls his spendings until it is paid off in full. That is reckoned a matter of honor.

Rusty Money

James, the first bishop of Jerusalem, had caught the Lord's very language as well as His thought. He said, "Your gold and silver are rusted, and their rust shall be for a testimony against you" (James 5:3). It would seem as though there was quite a bit of rusty money controlled by Christian people. It was lying in the ancient equivalents of vaults, and lands, and savings banks, and old stockings, gathering rust.

Money is in sore need. It needs friction, the friction of use. Without that its real, rare value will be completely lost. It is furnishing food for moths though it is meant to be furnishing spiritual food for men. There will be many a striking scene when some men come up into the Master's presence with loaded purses, "caught with the goods," while millions of their fellow men are living such pitiable lives because of their ignorance of Jesus.

But there are men who do understand. And their number is increasing. There are those who understand *the Master's basis* for conducting business matters. That basis is shrewd, faithful management of the business itself as good stewards of God; full, proper provision for home and loved ones—simple, but ample and intelligent; and then all the rest out in active service for men in Jesus' name. If that basis were more largely understood and accepted, what wondrous changes would come: changes out in the world, and changes in the home, and changes in the local church.

Many men are supporting their own representatives on the foreign field. Many a church now sustains its own missionary or missionaries. The ideal toward which the church might well aim is that *every family* should support its own national Christian worker overseas.[1] The real unit of life is the family. The children would then grow up with a vision for the world clearly and deeply marked in their minds. There are thousands of families in circumstances that could support a Christian worker by proper planning. The reflex blessing upon the home would be immeasurable in its sweetness and extent.

[1]World Literature Crusade currently sponsors over 1,800 full time literature distributors from more than fifty different evangelical denominations. For information on full or partial support of one of these national workers, write World Literature Crusade, P.O. Box 1313, Studio City, California 91604.

A Sacred Trust

Jesus admits us into the inner circle of friendship. He gives us the one rarest token of friendship, that is, a task to do for our Friend's sake. He asks us to go out to all men, and tell them about His love and sacrifice for them. And He asks that everything we have be held and used for this sacred trust. Are we being true to this sacred trust? Are we being true to our Friend's trust? Is there more stored away for ourselves than is being sent out on His errand? Is there any discoloration on our gold? Anything that looks like rust, a dull-red color? Ah, it looks strangely like the color—the stain—of blood.

Is Judas so lonely, after all? He coupled a token of friendship with a betrayal of his Friend's trust. Is he so much alone?

10

Sacrifice

A Lighthouse Candle

The light of a common candle in the window of a little cottage near the coast shone far out over the sea. It was up north of Scotland, in one of the Orkney Islands. Near the window sat a frail, grey-haired woman with cheery, thoughtful face. She was busy working at her spinning wheel, and watching the candle, turning now and again to trim it. All night long she sat at the spinning wheel and watched the candle. Fishermen out on the water, heading for home, knew that light could be counted on, and came safely in, past all the dangers of their coast.

For more than fifty years that woman tended her little lighthouse. When she was a young girl there had been a wild storm, and her father, out in his fishing boat, lost his life. There were no shore lights. His boat had struck a huge, dangerous rock called Lonely Rock, and been wrecked. The father's body was found in the morning, washed up on the shore. She had watched by her father's body, as was the habit of her people, until it was laid away. Then she lay down on her bed and slept the day through. When night came she rose, lit a candle, put it in the window, drew up her spinning wheel, and began her night vigil for the unknown out at sea.

All night long, and all her life long, her vigil of love and light continued. From youth to old age, through winter and summer, storm and calm, fog and clear, that humble lighthouse beacon failed not. Each night she spun so many spools of yarn for her daily bread, and one spool extra to purchase another candle. She turned night into day, reversing the whole habit of her life, and holding every other thing subject to her self-imposed task of love. And through the years many a fisherman out at sea, and many an anxious woman watching by hearth and crib, sent up heartfelt thanks to God for that little steady light. And many a life was saved, of which no record could be kept.

That tells the whole story of sacrifice: a need with nobody to meet it; the need passing into an emergency; the emergency turning into a tragedy; a heart sore torn to bleeding by the tragedy thrust bitterly home; then sacrifice, lifelong, that others might be saved where her loved one was lost, and still others spared what she herself suffered. And that story has been repeated with endless variations, and is being repeated, in every land, on every mission field, home and foreign.

Sin's Healing Shadow

Sacrifice has come to be a law of life. Wherever there is sin there will be a *call for sacrifice.* For sin makes need, and need intensifies into emergency. And need and emergency thrust someone into peril. And they call for sacrifice volunteered by someone, who would save the man in peril. And wherever there are true men and women, as well as need, there will *be* sacrifice.

And sin is everywhere. Even nature is full of evidence of a bad break in all its processes. The fingermarks of decay and death are below and above and all around its domain. That is sin's unmistakable earmark. Man's mental powers, and his loss of a full knowledge of his powers, tell the same story. And so there is need. Everywhere you turn need's pathetic face, drawn and white, looks piteously into yours, pleading mutely for help.

And so there is sacrifice. Sacrifice is sin's healing shadow. It follows sin at every turn, binding up its wounds, pouring in the oil and wine of its own life, and taking the hurt victims into its own warm heart. Nothing worthwhile has ever been done without sacrifice. *Every good thing done cost somebody his life.* The life may have been given out with a wrench under some sharp tug. Or it may have been given in a slower, more painful, more taxing and lingering way through years of steadfast doing or enduring.

Every man who has done something worthwhile for others has spilled some of his lifeblood into it. His work and name may have become known. Or he may belong to the large number of blessed faithfuls whose names are unknown here, but treasured faithfully above. Either way, the mark of his life is upon the thing he did. The nations that are freest cost most in the making, in the lives of men. Every church, and every mission station, has had to use red mortar as its walls went up.

Every bit of advance ground gained for liberty and truth has been stained with the lifeblood of the advance guard. You can depend upon it that whatever you are to do that will really help must have a bit of your own self, your very life in it. Immortality of action comes only by the infusion of human blood.

Sacrifice attends us faithfully from the cradle to the body's last resting place. The giving of one's self for others begins with the beginning of life, and never ends till life ends. Each of us came into life through the sacrifice of the mother who bore us. That love service of hers would not have been a sacrifice, but only a joy, had sin's cramping, restricting atmosphere not been breathed into all life. Now, with much pain, and great danger, and sometimes at the cost of life, it becomes a sacrifice of great sweet joy to her.

And that same spirit of sacrifice attends our baby years, and childhood experiences, and schooldays, and times of sickness, and our matured years. The more faithfully those who make up your life-circle yield to the law of sacrifice, and give of themselves out to you, the finer and stronger you grow to be, and the sweeter life becomes to you. And every selfish shirking and shrinking back by someone impoverishes your life by so much.

A hush of awe comes over our spirit as we recall that even for the Son of God there was no exception to this law, as He took His place down among human conditions. It was by His own blood that He saved men, and saves men. It was the spilling out of His own life that brings such blessed newness of life to us. His was a *living* sacrifice through all the years, and greatest when that life, so long being given, was given clean out.

That sacrifice of His stands unapproached, and can never be approached by any other. His relation to sin was different from that of all other men. He made a sacrifice for men in a sense that no other can. Yet, while that is true, it is equally true that every man who follows Him will drink of His cup of sacrifice.

But it is a cup of joy now, for His drinking drained out all the bitter dregs. He asks us into the inner fellowship of His suffering. *The work He began is not yet done.* He asks our help. We may fill up the measure of His sacrifice yet needed, in healing men's wounds and in throttling sin's power.

The Law of Sacrifice

The request of the Greek pilgrims, that last tragic week, drew out of Jesus wondrous words about the law of sacrifice (John 12: 24-26). Their request made the necessity for His coming sacrifice stand out more sharply in His mind—with edgy sharpness. The realness of that sacrifice of His stands out very vividly in the intensity of His feelings, of which we get only glimpses.

Listen to Him talking: "If the grain of wheat does not suffer death, it lives; but it lives alone. But through death it may live in the midst of a harvest of golden grains. The man who turns away from the appeal of need will live a lonely life, both here and in the longer life. [Is there anything more pathetic and pitiable than selfish loneliness!] He who feels the sharp tug of need, and cannot resist the appeal that calls for his lifeblood, rises up through that red pathway into blessed fellowship with the lives that owe their life to his."

He goes on: "He that clingeth with strong self-love to his life will find it slipping, slipping out of his fingers, leaving a dry husk of a shell in his tenacious clutch. But he who in the stress of the world's emergency of need, in the thick of the subtlest temptations to put the self-life first, treats that life as a hated enemy, to be opposed and fought, as he gives himself freely out to heal the world's hurt, *he* will find all the sweets and fragrance of life coming to him. Their unspeakable refreshment will ever increase, and never leave."

Then follow the words that go so deep: "If any man *would serve Me*, let him come along, putting his feet into My prints. Let him come through a long Nazareth life of common toil in home and shop, then along the crowded path of glad service for others, responding to every call of need. Let him come down into the shadowed olive grove beyond Kidron's waters, up that small hill outside a city wall, and deep down into the soil of men's needs.

"And where I am, there I will surely have that faithful follower of Mine up close by My side. He shall find himself rising up out of the common earth-life into a new life of strangely strong drawing power. And, while he will be all wrapped up in love's service, My Father will give special touches of His own hand upon his person, and upon his service."

In one of his exquisitely quiet talks, Henry Drummond used to tell the story of a famous statue in the Fine Arts Gallery of Paris. It was the work of a great genius, who, like many a genius, was very poor, and lived in a garret, which served as both studio and sleeping room.

One midnight, when the statue was just finished, a sudden frost fell upon Paris. The sculptor lay awake in his fireless garret, and thought of the still moist clay, thought how the moisture in the pores would freeze, and the dream of his life would be destroyed in a night. So the old man rose from his cot, wrapped his bedclothes reverently about the statue, and lay down to his sleep.

In the morning the neighbors found him lying dead. His life had gone out into his work. It was saved. He was gone. But he still lived in it, and still lives in it. He did not save his life, but he found a new life in the world of his art. He that saves his life shall surely lose it. He that gladly gives his life up for the Master's sake, and for men's sake, will find a wholly new life coming to him.

A Rare Harvest

There is a strange winsomeness about sacrifice, peculiar to itself, and peculiarly strong in its drawing power. Everywhere men acknowledge the peculiar fascination for them of the man who is not only wholly unselfish, but who utterly forgets himself in doing for others. The feeling is very common that the man in public life is chiefly concerned with what he can get out of it for himself. And when, now and then, the conviction seizes the crowd that some public man is not of that sort at all, but is devoting himself unselfishly and unsparingly to their interest, their admiration and love for him amount to a worship and enthusiasm that know no bounds.

There is something in unselfish sacrifice in their behalf that draws the crowd peculiarly and tremendously. Jesus said that once He was lifted up He would draw men. And He has. He was lifted up as none other, and He has been drawing men ever since as none other ever has or can. Quite apart from other truths involved, that sacrifice of His had in itself the tremendous drawing power of all unselfish action.

And sacrifice brews a subtle fragrance of its own that clings to the person like the soft sweet odor of wild roses. No one is ever conscious that there is any such fragrance going out to others. He knows the inner sweets that none know but they who give sacrifice brewing room within themselves. Such people do not stop to think about themselves, except to be thinking of helping and not hindering.

The very winsomeness of the sacrificial spirit has led men to the seeking of sacrifice. It seems strange to us that earnest men in other generations have sought by self-inflicted suffering to attain to the power that goes with sacrifice. And even yet some morbid people may be found following in their steps.

Do not they know that out in common daily life the knife of sacrifice is held across the path constantly, sharp edge out, barring the way? And no one can go faithfully his common round, with flag at masthead, and needs crowding in at front and rear and sides, without meeting its cutting edge. That edge cutting in as you push on frees out the fine fragrance. Whenever you meet a man or woman with that fine winsomeness of spirit that cannot be analyzed, but only felt, you may know that there has been some of this sort of sharp cutting within.

Blood is a rare fertilizer. They tell me that the bit of ground over in Belgium called Waterloo bears each spring a crop of rare blue forget-me-nots. That bit of ground had very unusual gardening. Plowed up by cannon and gunshot, sown deep with men's lives, "worked" thoroughly by toiling, struggling feet, moistened with the gentle rain of dying tears, and soaked with red life, it now yields its yearly harvest of beauty. All life is a Waterloo, and can be made to yield a rich growth of fragrant flowers.

The Fellowship of Scars

And there is yet more of this winsomeness. There is a spiritual power that flows out of sacrifice. It reaches far beyond the limited personal circle, out to the ends of the earth. It cannot be analyzed, nor defined, nor described, but it can be felt. We do not know much about the law of spirit-currents. But we know the spirit-currents themselves, for everyone is affected by them, and everyone is sending them out of himself.

You pick up a book, and suddenly find there is something in it that takes hold of you irresistibly. A flame seems to burn in it, and then in you. Invisible fingers seem to reach out of the page and play freely up and down the keyboard of your heart. Why is that? I do not know much about it. It is an elusive thing. But I can tell you my conviction, a conviction that grows stronger daily.

There is a life back of that book; there is sacrifice in that life of a keen, cutting sort; and Jesus is in that life, too, giving it His personal flavor. The life back of the book has come into the book. It is that life you are feeling as you read. Spirit power knows nothing about distance. The man who gives himself in sacrifice has a world-field, and is touching his field in a sense far greater than he ever knows.

And there is still more. The Master knows our sacrifices. He keenly notes the spirit that would give all, even as He did. He can breathe most of His own spirit into such a life. For it is most open to Him. He can do most through that spirit, for it comes nearest to His own. His own winsomeness breathes out of that life constantly.

Jesus knows every scar of sacrifice you bear, and loves it. For it tells Him your love. He knows the meaning of scars, because of His own. The marks of sacrifice cement our fellowship with Him. The nearer we come to fellowship with Him in the daily touch and spirit, the more freely can He reach out His own great winsomeness through us, out to His dear world.

"Won't You Please Save Me?"

To outsiders, who do not know about the matter, that word *sacrifice* has an ugly sound. It drives them away. But to the insiders, who have come in by the Jesus door, there is a joyousness of the bubbling-out, singing sort, that makes the word *sacrifice*, and the thing itself, forgotten even while remembered. It is remembered as a distinct and real thing, but it is pushed away from the center of your consciousness by this song that insists on singing its music into the ears of your heart.

I said a while ago in these talks that it would be *an easy thing* for the whole church, or even half of the church, to take Jesus fully out to all the world. But may I tell you now plainly that it will not be an easy thing? *Somebody will have to sacrifice if the thing is to be done.* And that somebody will be you, if you go along where the Master calls. If you *count* on the church's doing it, or on anybody else's doing it, you may be sure of one thing: some part of what needs doing will not be done.

But if you and I will reckon that this duty belongs to us, as if there were nobody else to do it, and *push on*—well, there will be sacrifice of the real sort and, too, there will be all of sacrifice's peculiar winsomeness going out to draw men. And there will be men changed where you live, and out where you will never go personally. And there will be a great joy in your heart, but with the greater joy breaking out in the morning, when the King comes to His own.

Years ago a steamer out on Lake Erie caught fire, and headed at once for the nearest land. All was wild confusion, as men and women struggled for means of escape. In the crowd was a California gold miner. He fastened the belt containing his gold securely about his waist, and was preparing to try to swim ashore. Just then a little sweet-faced girl in the crowd touched his hand, and looked up beseechingly into his face, and said, "Won't you please save me? I have no papa here to save me. Won't you, please?"

What would he do? He gave the belt of gold, that had meant such a hard struggle, one swift glance. But the child's soft touch on his hand, and that face and voice strangely affected him. He could not save both—which? All kinds of thoughts raced through his mind. Then he dropped the gold, and took the child, made the plunge, and by and by reached land, utterly exhausted, and lay unconscious. As his eyes opened, the child he had saved was standing over him with the tears of gratitude flooding her eyes. And a human life never seemed quite so precious. He had lost his gold, and his years of toil, but he had saved a life, and in saving it had found a new life springing up within him.

As we close our time together will you listen very softly. Listen: out of the distance comes a murmur of voices, like a low, long cry from the heart. It comes from nearby, where you live. It comes most from faraway lands. Its words are pathetically distinct: "*Will you help me?* I have no one to help me. Won't *you?*" And we can do it. But the gold and the life must go. *Shall* we do it, hand in hand with Jesus, the only Savior?

Shall we not do it?

Publisher's note:

Those interested in contacting World Literature Crusade for more information about its faith outreach through systematic literature distribution should write to:

Dr. Jack McAlister
World Literature Crusade
P.O. Box 1313
Studio City, CA 91604

In Canada:
Box 125
Prince Albert
Sask., S6V 5R4

In Australia:
Box 113
Hurstville, NSW 2220